REAL ESTATE LICENSE EXAM
Calculation Workbook

Coventry House Publishing

Copyright © 2022 Coventry House Publishing

All rights reserved.

ISBN: 1957426225
ISBN-13: 978-1957426228

CONTENTS

1 **Land Description and Development** 1
    Questions 3
    Answer Key 11

2 **Agency Agreements and Commissions** 15
    Questions 17
    Answer Key 25

3 **Mortgages and Finance** 29
    Questions 31
    Answer Key 39

4 **Appraising Real Estate Values** 43
    Questions 45
    Answer Key 49

5 **Taxation and Assessment** 51
    Questions 53
    Answer Key 59

6 **Real Estate Investment Analysis** 63
    Questions 65
    Answer Key 77

7 **Fundamental Math Concepts** 83
    Questions 85
    Answer Key 93

Index 99

SECTION 1

LAND DESCRIPTION AND DEVELOPMENT

QUESTIONS

1. Maria, a real estate developer, needs to earn $680,000 from the sale of lots in a subdivision to earn the required rate of return on her investment. The subdivision contains a total of 20 acres, and 15% of the land is to be used for roads. If each lot measures 1 acre, and no partial lots are permitted, Maria must charge _____ per lot to generate the required return.

   A. $40,000
   B. $45,000
   C. $50,000
   D. $55,000

2. Jacob purchased a parcel of land measuring one-fourth of a mile by one-fifth of a mile. The area of Jacob's land is:

   A. 28 acres.
   B. 30 acres.
   C. 32 acres.
   D. 34 acres.

3. Beta Corporation owns a 20-acre tract of land. To develop it, they must set aside 8% of the area for a pond, and 12% for streets and sidewalks. If the minimum permissible lot size is 8,000 square feet, the maximum number of lots that can be developed is:

   A. 82.
   B. 87.
   C. 91.
   D. 95.

4. Ken's lot sold for $190 a front foot. If the lot was 650 feet deep and had an area of 306,800 square feet, the selling price of his lot was:

   A. $78,760.
   B. $83,355.
   C. $89,680.
   D. $92,475.

5. Delta Real Estate Company purchased a 9-acre tract of land. If 10% of the land must be used for drainage and other uses, the maximum number of 10,000 square foot lots that can be platted is:

   A. 35.
   B. 38.
   C. 41.
   D. 44.

Land Description and Development

6. If a lot represents 28% of a square mile, the lot size is:

   A. 173.6 acres.
   B. 179.2 acres.
   C. 184.4 acres.
   D. 188.7 acres.

7. The number of square feet in 5 acres is:

   A. 209,600.
   B. 217,800.
   C. 226,900.
   D. 234,400.

8. Hannah sold her 3.2-acre lot for $820,000. The price per square foot was:

   A. $4.86.
   B. $5.21.
   C. $5.67.
   D. $5.88.

9. A parcel of land is square, measuring ½ mile by ½ mile. The number of acres in the parcel of land is:

   A. 160.
   B. 200.
   C. 240.
   D. 280.

10. Elaine purchased a 3.5-acre lot for $4 per square foot and built a house measuring 80 feet by 100 feet. If the price of the house was $150 per square foot, the total cost was:

    A. $1,762,450.
    B. $1,809,840.
    C. $1,913,680.
    D. $2,040,330.

11. Sigma Corporation is planning to develop a subdivision containing 150 lots averaging 20,000 square feet. If an average of 2,000 square feet of street, sidewalks, and drainage must be provided for each lot, the minimum number of acres the company will need to purchase to achieve their goal is:

    A. 75.76.
    B. 83.41.
    C. 94.58.
    D. 102.53.

Land Description and Development

12. Anna purchased a rectangular tract of land measuring 850 feet by 915 feet. The number of acres in the tract of land is:

    A. 15.90.
    B. 17.85.
    C. 19.55.
    D. 21.30.

13. Tom purchased three rectangular lots containing a total of 72,000 square feet. If each lot is 160 feet deep, then each of his lots has _____ of road frontage.

    A. 110 feet
    B. 130 feet
    C. 150 feet
    D. 170 feet

14. The number of acres in three townships is:

    A. 23,040.
    B. 46,080.
    C. 69,120.
    D. 92,160.

15. The area of two sections is:

    A. 1,280 acres.
    B. 1,920 acres.
    C. 2,560 acres.
    D. 3,200 acres.

16. If land has a perimeter of 18 miles on each side, the number of townships is:

    A. 6.
    B. 7.
    C. 8.
    D. 9.

17. Joanne owns a 10-acre plot of land that she would like to develop into lots measuring 120 feet by 200 feet. The maximum number of full lots that she can develop is:

    A. 14.
    B. 16.
    C. 18.
    D. 20.

Land Description and Development

The following information relates to questions 18 – 19.
Theta Development Company is subdividing a 6-acre tract of land into lots measuring 80 feet by 100 feet. They have allowed 53,360 square feet for streets and common areas.

18. Based on the information provided, the total number of lots that Theta Development Company can develop is:

    A. 26.
    B. 30.
    C. 34.
    D. 38.

19. Based on the information provided, if Theta Development Company plans to generate gross income of $1,300,000, they will need to sell each lot for:

    A. $40,000.
    B. $45,000.
    C. $50,000.
    D. $55,000.

20. A square area of land that measures 24 square miles can be described as a:

    A. township.
    B. quadrangle.
    C. half section.
    D. quarter section.

21. The number of acres in 4.5 square miles is:

    A. 2,240.
    B. 2,560.
    C. 2,880.
    D. 3,200.

22. Henry is selling the NW ¼, SW ½, S ½, W ¼ of a section. This is equivalent to:

    A. 390,400 square feet.
    B. 435,600 square feet.
    C. 476,200 square feet.
    D. 510,800 square feet.

23. The number of square feet in two sections is:

    A. 13,939,200.
    B. 27,878,400.
    C. 55,756,800.
    D. 83,635,200.

Land Description and Development

24. Jacqueline purchased a 1,550-square foot house on 1.2 acres of land. The price was $210 per square foot for the house plus $65,000 per acre. The total price paid by Jacqueline was:

A. $382,400.
B. $390,800.
C. $403,500.
D. $418,200.

The following information relates to questions 25 – 28.
Carl, a real estate developer, purchased a 20-acre tract of land. 15% of the land must be used for sidewalks and drainage, and zoning laws allow 2 lots per acre. Comparable lots are selling for $50,000, and 10% of the sale price of each lot must be allocated towards overhead and selling costs.

25. Based on the information provided, the total number of lots that Carl can develop is:

A. 22.
B. 26.
C. 30.
D. 34.

26. Based on the information provided, if all lots are sold, the gross sales price will be:

A. $1,500,000.
B. $1,700,000.
C. $1,900,000.
D. $2,100,000.

27. Based on the information provided, if all lots are sold, Carl's total overhead and selling costs will be:

A. $160,000.
B. $170,000.
C. $180,000.
D. $190,000.

28. Based on the information provided, if all lots are sold, Carl's profit will be:

A. $1,530,000.
B. $1,620,000.
C. $1,710,000.
D. $1,880,000.

Land Description and Development

29. Isaac, a real estate investor, owns a 36.25-acre lot. The lot represents _____ of a square mile.

   A. 4.82%
   B. 5.66%
   C. 6.48%
   D. 7.90%

30. Robin's property measures ¼ mile by ¼ mile. The area of her property is:

   A. 1,742,400 square feet.
   B. 3,484,800 square feet.
   C. 6,969,600 square feet.
   D. 13,939,200 square feet.

31. According to the guidelines of the Public Land Survey System, a township is approximately _____ square miles.

   A. 8
   B. 16
   C. 24
   D. 36

32. Lauren purchased 3 adjacent lots, each measuring 90 feet wide by 200 feet deep. If the total cost of the lots was $425,000, the price per square foot was:

   A. $7.09.
   B. $7.87.
   C. $8.63.
   D. $8.94.

33. Charles purchased a rectangular tract of land that contains 20 acres. If the measurement on one side is 1,800 feet, the depth of the land is:

   A. 484 feet.
   B. 592 feet.
   C. 636 feet.
   D. 758 feet.

34. Heather purchased a lot measuring 200 feet by 260 feet. If she paid $415,000 for the lot, the price per front foot was:

   A. $1,804.
   B. $1,966.
   C. $2,075.
   D. $2,125.

35. **Steve is selling a tract of land measuring 900 feet by 1,200 feet for $1,350,000. The price per acre is:**

   A. $43,835.
   B. $47,670.
   C. $51,325.
   D. $54,450.

ANSWER KEY

1. A
Step 1: Area for roads = 20 acres × 0.15 = 3 acres
Step 2: Remaining area for lots = 20 acres − 3 acres = 17 acres
Step 3: Number of lots = 17 acres ÷ 1 acre per lot = 17 lots
Step 4: Price per lot = $680,000 ÷ 17 lots = $40,000 per lot

2. C
Conversion factor 1: 1 mi. = 5,280 ft.
Conversion factor 2: 1 acre = 43,560 sq. ft.
Step 1: Area of lot (in square feet) = (5,280 ft. ÷ 4) × (5,280 ft. ÷ 5) = 1,393,920 sq. ft.
Step 2: Area of lot (in acres) = 1,393,920 sq. ft. ÷ 43,560 sq. ft. per acre = 32 acres

3. B
Conversion factor: 1 acre = 43,560 sq. ft.
Step 1: Area for pond = 20 acres × 0.08 = 1.6 acres
Step 2: Area for streets and sidewalks = 20 acres × 0.12 = 2.4 acres
Step 3: Remaining area for lots = 20 acres − 1.6 acres − 2.4 acres = 16 acres
Step 4: Square feet for lots = 16 acres × 43,560 sq. ft. per acre = 696,960 sq. ft.
Step 5: Number of lots = 606,960 sq. ft. ÷ 8,000 sq. ft. per lot = 87.12 = 87 full lots

4. C
Step 1: Width of lot = 306,800 sq. ft. ÷ 650 ft. = 472 ft.
Step 2: Selling price = $190 per ft. × 472 ft. = $89,680

5. A
Conversion factor: 1 acre = 43,560 sq. ft.
Step 1: Area for drainage and other uses = 9 acres × 0.1 = 0.9 acres
Step 2: Remaining area for lots = 9 acres − 0.9 acres = 8.1 acres
Step 3: Square feet for lots = 8.1 acres × 43,560 sq. ft. per acre = 352,836 sq. ft.
Step 4: Number of lots = 352,836 sq. ft. ÷ 10,000 sq. ft. per lot = 35.3 = 35 full lots

6. B
Conversion factor: 1 sq. mi. = 640 acres
Lot size = 640 acres × 0.28 = 179.2 acres

7. B
Conversion factor: 1 acre = 43,560 sq. ft.
Number of square feet = 5 acres × 43,560 sq. ft. per acre = 217,800 sq. ft.

8. D
Conversion factor: 1 acre = 43,560 sq. ft.
Step 1: Area of lot = 3.2 acres × 43,560 sq. ft. per acre = 139,392 sq. ft.
Step 2: Price per square foot = $820,000 ÷ 139,392 sq. ft. = $5.88 per sq. ft.

9. A
Conversion factor: 1 sq. mi. = 640 acres
Step 1: Area of land = 0.5 mi. × 0.5 mi. = 0.25 sq. mi.
Step 2: Number of acres = 640 acres per sq. mi. × 0.25 sq. mi. = 160 acres

10. B
Conversion factor: 1 acre = 43,560 sq. ft.
Step 1: Cost of lot = 3.5 acres × 43,560 sq. ft. per acre × $4 per sq. ft. = $609,840
Step 2: Area of house = 80 ft. × 100 ft. = 8,000 sq. ft.
Step 3: Cost of house = 8,000 sq. ft. × $150 per sq. ft. = $1,200,000
Step 4: Total cost = $609,840 + $1,200,000 = $1,809,840

11. A
Conversion factor: 1 acre = 43,560 sq. ft.
Step 1: Required square feet per lot = 20,000 sq. ft. + 2,000 sq. ft. = 22,000 sq. ft. per lot
Step 2: Area of lots = 150 lots × 22,000 sq. ft. per lot = 3,300,000 sq. ft.
Step 3: Number of acres = 3,300,000 sq. ft. ÷ 43,560 sq. ft. per acre = 75.76 acres

12. B
Conversion factor: 1 acre = 43,560 sq. ft.
Step 1: Area of land = 850 ft. × 915 ft. = 777,750 sq. ft.
Step 2: Number of acres = 777,750 sq. ft. ÷ 43,560 sq. ft. per acre = 17.85 acres

13. C
If each lot is rectangular and has the same depth, then each lot has the same width.
Step 1: Area of each lot = 72,000 sq. ft. ÷ 3 lots = 24,000 sq. ft. per lot
Step 2: Road frontage of each lot = 24,000 sq. ft. per lot ÷ 160 ft. = 150 ft. per lot

14. C
Conversion factor 1: 1 township = 36 sq. mi.
Conversion factor 2: 1 sq. mi. = 640 acres
Number of acres = 3 × 36 sq. mi. × 640 acres per sq. mi. = 69,120 acres

15. A
Conversion factor 1: 1 section = 1 mi. × 1 mi.
Conversion factor 2: 1 mi. = 5,280 ft.
Conversion factor 3: 1 acre = 43,560 sq. ft.
Step 1: Area of section (in square feet) = 5,280 ft. × 5,280 ft. = 27,878,400 sq. ft.
Step 2: Area of section (in acres) = 27,878,400 sq. ft. ÷ 43,560 sq. ft. per acre = 640 acres
Step 3: Total area = 2 sections × 640 acres per section = 1,280 acres

16. D
Conversion factor: 1 township = 36 sq. mi.
Step 1: Area of land = 18 mi. × 18 mi. = 324 sq. mi.
Step 2: Number of townships = 324 sq. mi. ÷ 36 sq. mi. per township = 9 townships

17. C
Conversion factor: 1 acre = 43,560 sq. ft.
Step 1: Area of land = 10 acres × 43,560 sq. ft. per acre = 435,600 sq. ft.
Step 2: Area of each lot = 120 ft. × 200 ft. = 24,000 sq. ft. per lot
Step 3: Number of lots = 435,600 sq. ft. ÷ 24,000 sq. ft. per lot = 18.15 = 18 full lots

Land Description and Development

18. A
Conversion factor: 1 acre = 43,560 sq. ft.
Step 1: Area of land = 6 acres × 43,560 sq. ft. per acre = 261,360 sq. ft.
Step 2: Remaining area for lots = 261,360 sq. ft. − 53,360 sq. ft. = 208,000 sq. ft.
Step 3: Area of each lot = 80 ft. × 100 ft. = 8,000 sq. ft. per lot
Step 4: Number of lots = 208,000 sq. ft. ÷ 8,000 sq. ft. per lot = 26 lots

19. C
Conversion factor: 1 acre = 43,560 sq. ft.
Step 1: Area of land = 6 acres × 43,560 sq. ft. per acre = 261,360 sq. ft.
Step 2: Remaining area for lots = 261,360 sq. ft. − 53,360 sq. ft. = 208,000 sq. ft.
Step 3: Area of each lot = 80 ft. × 100 ft. = 8,000 sq. ft. per lot
Step 4: Number of lots = 208,000 sq. ft. ÷ 8,000 sq. ft. per lot = 26 lots
Step 5: Price per lot = $1,300,000 ÷ 26 lots = $50,000 per lot

20. B
A quadrangle is a square area of land that is 24 miles on each side or 576 square miles.

21. C
Conversion factor: 1 sq. mi. = 640 acres
Number of acres = 4.5 sq. mi. × 640 acres per sq. mi. = 2,880 acres

22. B
Conversion factor 1: 1 section = 640 acres
Conversion factor 2: 1 acre = 43,560 sq. ft.
Step 1: Area of land (in acres) = 640 acres × ¼ × ½ × ½ × ¼ = 10 acres
Step 2: Area of land (in square feet) = 10 acres × 43,560 sq. ft. per acre = 435,600 sq. ft.

23. C
Conversion factor 1: 1 section = 1 mi. × 1 mi.
Conversion factor 2: 1 mi. = 5,280 ft.
Area of two sections = 2 × 5,280 ft. × 5,280 ft. = 55,756,800 sq. ft.

24. C
Step 1: Cost of house = 1,550 sq. ft. × $210 per sq. ft. = $325,500
Step 2: Cost of lot = 1.2 acres × $65,000 per acre = $78,000
Step 3: Total cost = $325,500 + $78,000 = $403,500

25. D
Step 1: Area for sidewalks and drainage = 20 acres × 0.15 = 3 acres
Step 2: Remaining area for lots = 20 acres − 3 acres = 17 acres
Step 3: Number of lots = 17 acres × 2 lots per acre = 34 lots

26. B
Step 1: Area for sidewalks and drainage = 20 acres × 0.15 = 3 acres
Step 2: Remaining area for lots = 20 acres − 3 acres = 17 acres
Step 3: Number of lots = 17 acres × 2 lots per acre = 34 lots
Step 4: Gross sales price = 34 lots × $50,000 per lot = $1,700,000

Land Description and Development

27. B
Step 1: Area for sidewalks and drainage = 20 acres × 0.15 = 3 acres
Step 2: Remaining area for lots = 20 acres − 3 acres = 17 acres
Step 3: Number of lots = 17 acres × 2 lots per acre = 34 lots
Step 4: Gross sales price = 34 lots × $50,000 per lot = $1,700,000
Step 5: Overhead and selling costs = $1,700,000 × 0.1 = $170,000

28. A
Step 1: Area for sidewalks and drainage = 20 acres × 0.15 = 3 acres
Step 2: Remaining area for lots = 20 acres − 3 acres = 17 acres
Step 3: Number of lots = 17 acres × 2 lots per acre = 34 lots
Step 4: Gross sales price = 34 lots × $50,000 per lot = $1,700,000
Step 5: Overhead and selling costs = $1,700,000 × 0.1 = $170,000
Step 6: Potential profit = $1,700,000 − $170,000 = $1,530,000

29. B
Conversion factor: 1 sq. mi. = 640 acres
Percentage of a square mile = 36.25 acres ÷ 640 acres = 0.0566 = 5.66%

30. A
Conversion factor: 1 mi. = 5,280 ft.
Area of property = (5,280 ft. ÷ 4) × (5,280 ft. ÷ 4) = 1,742,400 sq. ft.

31. D
According to the guidelines of the Public Land Survey System, a township is approximately 36 square miles.

32. B
Step 1: Area of each lot = 90 ft. × 200 ft. = 18,000 sq. ft. per lot
Step 2: Total area = 18,000 sq. ft. per lot × 3 lots = 54,000 sq. ft.
Step 3: Price per square foot = $425,000 ÷ 54,000 sq. ft. = $7.87 per sq. ft.

33. A
Conversion factor: 1 acre = 43,560 sq. ft.
Step 1: Area of land = 20 acres × 43,560 sq. ft. per acre = 871,200 sq. ft.
Step 2: Depth of land = 871,200 sq. ft. ÷ 1,800 ft. = 484 ft.

34. C
Price per front foot = $415,000 ÷ 200 ft. = $2,075 per ft.

35. D
Conversion factor: 1 acre = 43,560 sq. ft.
Step 1: Area of land = 900 ft. × 1,200 ft. = 1,080,000 sq. ft.
Step 2: Number of acres = 1,080,000 sq. ft. ÷ 43,560 sq. ft. per acre = 24.7934 acres
Step 3: Price per acre = $1,350,000 ÷ 24.7934 acres = $54,450 per acre

SECTION 2

AGENCY AGREEMENTS AND COMMISSIONS

QUESTIONS

1. A house sold for $920,000 with a 6% commission. The listing broker paid the selling broker 50%. The listing salesperson and the selling salesperson each received 50% of what their brokers received. The selling salesperson received:

   A. $13,800.
   B. $20,700.
   C. $27,600.
   D. $41,400.

2. Andrew, a broker with a 6% commission rate, is calculating the listing price for his client's house. If the value of the lot is $95,000 net of commission, and the value of the house is $245,000 net of commission, the approximate listing price should be:

   A. $253,508.
   B. $257,694.
   C. $361,702.
   D. $365,431.

3. Taylor sold her client's house for $150,000, which represents a 20% decrease from the original listing price. If Taylor receives 5% of the final sale price, she would have earned _____ if the house had sold for its original price.

   A. $7,500
   B. $8,435
   C. $9,375
   D. $10,300

4. A 20-acre property sold for $85,000 per acre with a 5.5% commission. If the listing broker and selling broker will split the commission evenly, each broker will receive:

   A. $46,750.
   B. $49,310.
   C. $52,480.
   D. $55,190.

5. A broker pays his salesperson, Julie, 40% of the first $100,000 of total gross commissions received each year, and 60% of the amount in excess of $100,000. If Julie generated $400,000 in total gross commissions, she will earn:

   A. $180,000.
   B. $200,000.
   C. $220,000.
   D. $240,000.

Agency Agreements and Commissions

6. A farm was listed for $650,000 and sold for $630,000. The seller's closing costs were 3%, and the broker's commission was 6.5%. If the mortgage balance at the time of the sale was $405,000, the seller received _____ in cash at closing.

A. $165,150
B. $189,475
C. $196,320
D. $203,905

7. Eric would like to net at least $615,000 from the sale of his house. If his closing costs will be $23,900, and the broker's commission rate is 5.5%, the gross sales price of his house should be greater than:

A. $648,825.
B. $650,794.
C. $674,040.
D. $676,085.

8. Mark, a sales representative, is required to pay $1,100 per month to the broker for use of office space, and he receives 40% of commissions brought in. Last month, if Mark received a net payment of $3,600, the amount of commissions that he collected was:

A. $2,500.
B. $4,700.
C. $5,600.
D. $7,200.

9. Brittany, a broker, listed a property for $385,000 at a 6% commission rate. If the eventual sales price was $378,200, her commission was _____ less than it would have been if the property had sold at the listed price.

A. $366
B. $408
C. $514
D. $602

10. Amelia, a broker, shares the commission that is earned on the sale of real estate with her salesperson in a 5 to 3 ratio, respectively. If the salesperson sells a property for $400,000 at a 5% commission rate, then Amelia will earn _____ more than the salesperson.

A. $5,000
B. $10,000
C. $15,000
D. $20,000

Agency Agreements and Commissions

The following information relates to questions 11 – 12.
A broker keeps 55% of sales commissions and pays her salesperson the remaining 45%. Last month the salesperson sold 10 acres of land at $25,000 per acre, with a gross commission rate of 6%.

11. Based on the information provided, the broker earned:

    A. $8,250.
    B. $11,625.
    C. $13,312.
    D. $15,000.

12. Based on the information provided, the salesperson earned:

    A. $6,500.
    B. $6,750.
    C. $7,250.
    D. $7,500.

13. Joel sold his house and paid a 5.5% commission and 2.5% of the selling price in closing costs. If he received net proceeds of $460,000, the gross sales price of his house was:

    A. $470,000.
    B. $480,000.
    C. $490,000.
    D. $500,000.

14. Emma received net proceeds of $336,400 from the sale of her house. If she paid $9,520 in closing costs in addition to a 6% commission, the gross sales price of her house was:

    A. $358,000.
    B. $366,000.
    C. $368,000.
    D. $374,000.

15. Alexander, a salesperson, receives 70% of the first $25,000 of commissions that he brings in and 60% of the amount in excess of $25,000. If his real estate sales totaled $1,500,000 last year, and his commission rate was 5%, then Alexander received a payout of:

    A. $45,000.
    B. $46,750.
    C. $47,500.
    D. $48,250.

Agency Agreements and Commissions

The following information relates to questions 16 – 17.
A salesperson associated with a broker listed a house for $715,000 with a 6% commission. A month later, the homeowner accepted an offer of $680,000, solicited by the salesperson. The broker's practice is that 45% of commissions are retained by the office and the remainder is paid to the salesperson.

16. Based on the information provided, the salesperson's payout will be:

   A. $14,160.
   B. $22,440.
   C. $31,620.
   D. $40,800.

17. Based on the information provided, the office will retain:

   A. $18,360.
   B. $24,180.
   C. $32,730.
   D. $40,800.

18. Adam, a broker, has a listing that requires a 6% brokerage commission. Adam offers 50% of the commission to the selling broker, Claire. If Adam sells the property for $915,200, the seller must pay him:

   A. $27,456.
   B. $41,184.
   C. $54,912.
   D. $82,368.

19. If Nick is selling his house and wants to net $405,000 from the sale after paying a 5% commission, his house must sell for:

   A. $384,750.
   B. $405,000.
   C. $414,524.
   D. $426,316.

20. Grace, a listing broker, will receive a commission of 5% on the first $250,000 of a property's sale price, and 4% on any amount over $250,000. If a property sells for $400,000, Grace's commission will be:

   A. $16,900.
   B. $17,800.
   C. $18,500.
   D. $19,200.

Agency Agreements and Commissions

21. Charlotte's house was listed for $675,000 and sold for $640,000. If the listing broker split the 6% commission evenly with the selling broker, the listing broker's commission was:

A. $9,600.
B. $19,200.
C. $28,800.
D. $38,400.

The following information relates to questions 22 – 23.
Susan recently sold her house and received a check for $245,000 after paying $5,000 in closing costs and a 6% commission.

22. Based on the information provided, the gross sales price of Susan's house was:

A. $260,461.
B. $265,957.
C. $270,308.
D. $275,249.

23. Based on the information provided, the commission was:

A. $15,957.
B. $16,736.
C. $17,924.
D. $18,405.

24. Luke purchased a property for $550,000. Three years later, he sold the property for $595,000 and paid a broker's commission of 5%. Luke's rate of profit after paying the commission was:

A. 2.77%.
B. 3.08%.
C. 3.66%.
D. 4.14%.

25. Jeff, a broker, has agreed to pay his salesperson one-fifth of all commissions earned as a result of the salesperson's efforts. If the salesperson sells a property for $510,000 with a 5% commission rate, then Jeff's share of the commission is:

A. $5,100.
B. $18,600.
C. $20,400.
D. $24,200.

Agency Agreements and Commissions

The following information relates to questions 26 – 27.
Russell referred a client to Beth, who sold the client a house for $900,000. Beth paid Russell a referral fee equal to 7% of her commission. Russell received $3,150 from Beth.

26. Based on the information provided, Beth's commission was:

A. $3,150.
B. $40,000.
C. $45,000.
D. $63,000.

27. Based on the information provided, Beth's commission rate was:

A. 4%.
B. 5%.
C. 6%.
D. 7%.

28. After paying a 6.5% commission, Cole received net proceeds of $481,525 from the sale of his house. The gross sales price was:

A. $450,000.
B. $462,000.
C. $512,000.
D. $515,000.

29. Jane, a broker, sold her client's house for $755,000. If her commission rate was 4.5%, her commission was:

A. $31,465.
B. $33,975.
C. $35,620.
D. $37,850.

30. Graham, a broker, sold his client's house and received a 5% commission, which was equal to $22,500. The gross sales price of the house was:

A. $435,000.
B. $440,000.
C. $445,000.
D. $450,000.

31. Lori, a broker, sold an office building for $2,865,200. If her commission rate was 6% and she received 50% of the total sales commission, her payout was:

A. $70,693.
B. $75,352.
C. $80,460.
D. $85,956.

Agency Agreements and Commissions

32. Leah, a broker, will receive a commission of 5% on the first $100,000 of a property's sale price, 4% on the next $100,000, and 3% for the remainder. If Leah sells her client's house for $750,000, her commission will be:

    A. $21,500.
    B. $23,000.
    C. $25,500.
    D. $27,000.

33. Larry, a salesperson, receives 65% of the total commission on a property that sold for $365,000. If he received $11,856, his rate of commission was:

    A. 3%.
    B. 4%.
    C. 5%.
    D. 6%.

The following information relates to questions 34 – 35.
Tony, a salesperson, works for a broker. Tony receives 40% of all commissions that he brings in. He recently sold a house for $750,000 at a 6% commission rate.

34. Based on the information provided, Tony's share of the proceeds is:

    A. $9,000.
    B. $18,000.
    C. $27,000.
    D. $36,000.

35. Based on the information provided, the broker's share of the proceeds is:

    A. $9,000.
    B. $18,000.
    C. $27,000.
    D. $36,000.

ANSWER KEY

1. A
Step 1: Total commission = $920,000 × 0.06 = $55,200
Step 2: Broker's payout = $55,200 × 0.5 = $27,600
Step 3: Salesperson's payout = $27,600 × 0.5 = $13,800

2. C
Listing price = ($95,000 + $245,000) ÷ (1 − 0.06) = $361,702

3. C
Step 1: Original listing price = $150,000 ÷ (1 − 0.2) = $187,500
Step 2: Commission = $187,500 × 0.05 = $9,375

4. A
Step 1: Total sales price = 20 acres × $85,000 per acre = $1,700,000
Step 2: Total commission = $1,700,000 × 0.055 = $93,500
Step 3: Each broker's commission = $93,500 × 0.5 = $46,750

5. C
Step 1: Payout on the first $100,000 = $100,000 × 0.4 = $40,000
Step 2: Payout on amount over $100,000 = ($400,000 − $100,000) × 0.6 = $180,000
Step 3: Total payout = $40,000 + $180,000 = $220,000

6. A
Step 1: Closing costs = $630,000 × 0.03 = $18,900
Step 2: Broker's commission = $630,000 × 0.065 = $40,950
Step 3: Equity in farm = $630,000 − $405,000 = $225,000
Step 4: Cash received at closing = $225,000 − $18,900 − $40,950 = $165,150

7. D
Gross sales price = ($615,000 + $23,900) ÷ (1 − 0.055) = $676,085

8. B
Commission collected = $3,600 + $1,100 = $4,700

9. B
Step 1: List price commission = $385,000 × 0.06 = $23,100
Step 2: Sale price commission = $378,200 × 0.06 = $22,692
Step 3: Difference = $23,100 − $22,692 = $408

10. A
Step 1: Total commission = $400,000 × 0.05 = $20,000
Step 2: Broker's payout = $20,000 × 5/8 = $12,500
Step 3: Salesperson's payout = $20,000 × 3/8 = $7,500
Step 4: Difference = $12,500 − $7,500 = $5,000

Agency Agreements and Commissions

11. A
Step 1: Total sales price = 10 acres × $25,000 per acre = $250,000
Step 2: Total commission = $250,000 × 0.06 = $15,000
Step 3: Broker's payout = $15,000 × 0.55 = $8,250

12. B
Step 1: Total sales price = 10 acres × $25,000 per acre = $250,000
Step 2: Total commission = $250,000 × 0.06 = $15,000
Step 3: Salesperson's payout = $15,000 × 0.45 = $6,750

13. D
Gross sales price = $460,000 ÷ (1 − 0.055 − 0.025) = $500,000

14. C
Gross sales price = ($336,400 + $9,520) ÷ (1 − 0.06) = $368,000

15. C
Step 1: Total commission = $1,500,000 × 0.05 = $75,000
Step 2: Payout on the first $25,000 = $25,000 × 0.7 = $17,500
Step 3: Payout on amount over $25,000 = ($75,000 − $25,000) × 0.6 = $30,000
Step 4: Total payout = $17,500 + $30,000 = $47,500

16. B
Step 1: Total commission = $680,000 × 0.06 = $40,800
Step 2: Salesperson's payout = $40,800 × (1 − 0.45) = $22,440

17. A
Step 1: Total commission = $680,000 × 0.06 = $40,800
Step 2: Earnings retained by office = $40,800 × 0.45 = $18,360

18. C
Broker's commission = $915,200 × 0.06 = $54,912

19. D
Sale price = $405,000 ÷ (1 − 0.05) = $426,316

20. C
Step 1: Commission on the first $250,000 = $250,000 × 0.05 = $12,500
Step 2: Commission over $250,000 = ($400,000 − $250,000) × 0.04 = $6,000
Step 3: Total commission = $12,500 + $6,000 = $18,500

21. B
Step 1: Total commission = $640,000 × 0.06 = $38,400
Step 2: Listing broker's commission = $38,400 × 0.5 = $19,200

22. B
Gross sales price = ($245,000 + $5,000) ÷ (1 − 0.06) = $265,957

Agency Agreements and Commissions

23. A
Step 1: Gross sales price = ($245,000 + $5,000) ÷ (1 − 0.06) = $265,957
Step 2: Commission = $265,957 × 0.06 = $15,957

24. A
Step 1: Net sales price = $595,000 × (1 − 0.05) = $565,250
Step 2: Rate of profit = ($565,250 − $550,000) ÷ $550,000 = 0.0277 = 2.77%

25. C
Step 1: Total commission = $510,000 × 0.05 = $25,500
Step 2: Broker's commission = $25,500 × 0.8 = $20,400
(The remaining $5,100 will be paid to the salesperson.)

26. C
Beth's commission = $3,150 ÷ 0.07 = $45,000

27. B
Step 1: Beth's commission = $3,150 ÷ 0.07 = $45,000
Step 2: Beth's commission rate = $45,000 ÷ $900,000 = 0.05 = 5%

28. D
Gross sales price = $481,525 ÷ (1 − 0.065) = $515,000

29. B
Commission = $755,000 × 0.045 = $33,975

30. D
Gross sales price = $22,500 ÷ 0.05 = $450,000

31. D
Step 1: Total commission: $2,865,200 × 0.06 = $171,912
Step 2: Broker's payout: $171,912 × 0.5 = $85,956

32. C
Step 1: Commission on the first $100,000 = $100,000 × 0.05 = $5,000
Step 2: Commission on the next $100,000 = $100,000 × 0.04 = $4,000
Step 3: Commission over $200,000 = ($750,000 − $200,000) × 0.03 = $16,500
Step 4: Total commission = $5,000 + $4,000 + $16,500 = $25,500

33. C
Step 1: Salesperson's commission = $11,856 ÷ 0.65 = $18,240
Step 2: Salesperson's commission rate = $18,240 ÷ $365,000 = 0.05 = 5%

34. B
Step 1: Total commission = $750,000 × 0.06 = $45,000
Step 2: Salesperson's payout = $45,000 × 0.4 = $18,000

35. C
Step 1: Total commission = $750,000 × 0.06 = $45,000
Step 2: Broker's payout = $45,000 × (1 − 0.4) = $27,000

SECTION 3

MORTGAGES AND FINANCE

QUESTIONS

1. Ethan has an annual income of $125,000. A mortgage lender will provide a loan equal to 3 times annual income. If Ethan makes a 15% down payment, the maximum house that he can afford to purchase is:

   A. $438,284.
   B. $441,176.
   C. $444,592.
   D. $447,308.

2. Logan's mortgage balance is $150,000 and carries a 5% interest rate. If monthly payments are $805, the principal will be reduced by _____ from the first payment.

   A. $172
   B. $176
   C. $180
   D. $184

3. Katie owns a warehouse with a current value of $550,000. Jared owns a building with a current value of $800,000 and a $150,000 mortgage balance. If Katie assumes the mortgage, a fair trade would require:

   A. Katie to pay $75,000 cash.
   B. Katie to pay $100,000 cash.
   C. Jared to pay $125,000 cash.
   D. Jared to pay $150,000 cash.

4. Roger acquires a 15-year mortgage with a balance of $270,000. If the interest rate is 4.8%, and he pays back the mortgage using level principal payments each month, the payment for the first month will be:

   A. $1,970.
   B. $2,140.
   C. $2,310.
   D. $2,580.

5. Gamma Mortgage Company's underwriting requirements specify a maximum housing debt-to-income ratio of 25%. If the applicant discloses annual earnings of $92,000, the maximum monthly PITI payment the mortgage company will accept is:

   A. $958.33.
   B. $1,916.67.
   C. $3,833.33.
   D. $5,165.50.

Mortgages and Finance

6. Celine would like to purchase a house for $615,000. If she pays $10,000 in earnest money and applies for a mortgage equal to 75% of the purchase price, then she will need to pay _____ to meet the requirements of the mortgage.

   A. $133,050
   B. $138,550
   C. $143,750
   D. $148,250

7. The seller has agreed to pay 2 points to the mortgage company to help the buyer obtain a mortgage. The house was listed for $500,000 and is being sold for $485,000. If the buyer will pay 10% in cash and borrow the remaining amount, the seller will owe _____ to the lender for points.

   A. $8,230
   B. $8,730
   C. $9,000
   D. $9,700

8. If George's mortgage balance is $288,000 and requires a payment of $1,200 each month in interest, the annual interest rate is:

   A. 4.5%.
   B. 5.0%.
   C. 5.5%.
   D. 6.0%.

9. Bailey's mortgage has an interest rate of 6.6%. If the interest payable for the current month is $2,104.25, the mortgage balance at the beginning of the month was:

   A. $318,825.76.
   B. $341,314.67.
   C. $382,590.91.
   D. $399,509.26.

10. Devin obtained an interest-only mortgage with a balance of $620,000 and a 5.7% interest rate. The term of the mortgage is 30 years, including the interest-only period of 5 years. The amount of interest Devin will have paid after the first 9 months of the mortgage is:

    A. $25,470.
    B. $26,505.
    C. $27,825.
    D. $28,360.

Mortgages and Finance

11. Rachel is selling her house and the closing date is March 28. Interest is payable, with the payment due on the 15th of the month. The loan amount as of March 15 is $220,000, and the annual interest rate is 6%. If the loan is assumed, Rachel will have to pay the buyer _____ in prorated interest.

    A. $496.72
    B. $503.86
    C. $512.44
    D. $527.39

12. Alan is purchasing a condo for $450,000. If the mortgage requires a 15% down payment, a 0.75% private mortgage insurance (PMI) fee, and a 1.5% origination fee, the total amount that Alan will have to pay is:

    A. $75,412.61.
    B. $76,106.25.
    C. $77,610.59.
    D. $78,406.02.

13. The seller has agreed to pay 2.5 points to the mortgage company to help the buyer obtain a mortgage. If the house is being sold for $410,000, and the buyer will pay 30% in cash and borrow the remaining amount, the seller will owe _____ to the lender for points.

    A. $4,225
    B. $5,520
    C. $7,175
    D. $10,250

14. Fred acquired a 15-year mortgage in the amount of $500,000. If the interest rate is 6%, the principal balance after the first monthly payment of $4,219.28 is:

    A. $495,894.31.
    B. $496,521.07.
    C. $497,683.19.
    D. $498,280.72.

15. Kelly is purchasing a house for $395,000. If she's made an earnest money deposit of $3,500, and the lender has agreed to provide a mortgage equal to 75% of the sale price, the amount of additional cash that she must pay in order to meet the requirements of the loan is:

    A. $91,750.
    B. $95,250.
    C. $98,750.
    D. $102,250.

Mortgages and Finance

The following information relates to questions 16 – 17.
Lindsey obtained a 30-year mortgage with a current balance of $390,000. The interest rate on the mortgage is 5.4% and monthly payments are $2,190.

16. Based on the information provided, the interest payment in the first month will be:

   A. $1,590.
   B. $1,685.
   C. $1,755.
   D. $1,840.

17. Based on the information provided, the principal payment in the first month will be:

   A. $390.
   B. $405.
   C. $420.
   D. $435.

18. Jake is obtaining a mortgage with closing costs equal to 2 discount points. If the property is valued at $130,000, and the mortgage is 75% of the property's value, then Jake must pay closing costs of:

   A. $1,625.
   B. $1,950.
   C. $2,275.
   D. $2,600.

19. Audrey obtained a 30-year mortgage in the amount of $770,000. If the interest rate is 6.15% and monthly payments are $4,691.06, the total interest paid over the life of the mortgage is:

   A. $770,000.00.
   B. $824,626.12.
   C. $918,781.60.
   D. $1,688,781.35.

20. Kristina has an annual income of $150,000. She is applying for a mortgage, and the lender will provide a loan up to 4 times annual income. If Kristina makes a 25% down payment, the maximum house that she can afford to purchase is:

   A. $600,000.
   B. $800,000.
   C. $900,000.
   D. $1,000,000.

21. Dan acquired a 20-year mortgage with a beginning balance of $285,290. If the interest rate is 5.25% and monthly payments are $1,922.41, then the total interest paid if the mortgage runs to maturity is:

   A. $159,210.24.
   B. $165,465.91.
   C. $176,088.40.
   D. $183,921.53.

22. Kevin has an annual income of $225,000. If he wants to keep his PITI payments at or below 25% of his income, and he also wants to keep his total debt payments at or below 35% of his income, the maximum monthly PITI payment that he can afford is:

   A. $3,496.70.
   B. $3,825.10.
   C. $4,238.20.
   D. $4,687.50.

23. Oscar is purchasing a house with a current value of $620,000. If he will acquire a mortgage equal to 80% of the house value, and he has already paid $15,500 in earnest money, then he must pay _____ to meet the requirements of the loan.

   A. $93,000
   B. $108,500
   C. $124,000
   D. $139,500

The following information relates to questions 24 – 25.
Julia has a 15-year mortgage with a current balance of $600,000 and an interest rate of 6.25%. Her house was recently appraised for $1,500,000.

24. Based on the information provided, the equity in Julia's house is:

   A. $600,000.
   B. $800,000.
   C. $900,000.
   D. $1,500,000.

25. Based on the information provided, Julia's debt-to-equity ratio is:

   A. 1:4.
   B. 2:3.
   C. 3:2.
   D. 4:1.

Mortgages and Finance

26. Scott is purchasing a house for $515,000. If the appraised value is $500,000, and the bank offers an 80% loan-to-value ratio, his required down payment will be:

    A. $100,000.
    B. $103,000.
    C. $115,000.
    D. $118,000.

27. Vanessa received a home loan in the amount of $671,595. If the annual interest rate is 5.125%, the amount of interest that she will owe in the first year is:

    A. $2,868.27.
    B. $17,209.62.
    C. $34,419.24.
    D. $37,524.36.

28. If mortgage interest for the current month is $950, and the interest rate is 5.1%, then the principal balance is:

    A. $223,529.41.
    B. $224,686.57.
    C. $225,377.39.
    D. $226,804.26.

29. If Kyle's annual income is $88,000, then his monthly mortgage payment of $950 represents _____ of his annual income.

    A. 1%
    B. 6%
    C. 11%
    D. 13%

30. Cody obtained a 30-year mortgage with a balance of $1,200,000. If the interest rate is 6.15%, the first month's interest payment will be:

    A. $5,500.
    B. $5,700.
    C. $5,950.
    D. $6,150.

31. Natalie is purchasing land for $565,000 and applying for a mortgage. If the lender requires a 65% loan-to-value ratio, Natalie's down payment will need to be:

    A. $178,875.
    B. $197,750.
    C. $236,625.
    D. $367,250.

Mortgages and Finance

The following information relates to questions 32 – 35.
Jen purchased a house for $250,000 and obtained a 30-year fixed rate mortgage in the amount of $200,000. The interest rate on the mortgage is 6% and the monthly payment is $1,199.

32. Based on the information provided, the amount of interest that will be paid during the first year is:

    A. $8,000.
    B. $10,000.
    C. $12,000.
    D. $14,000.

33. Based on the information provided, the amount of interest that will be paid in the first month is:

    A. $1,000.
    B. $1,500.
    C. $2,000.
    D. $2,500.

34. Based on the information provided, the amount of principal that will be paid in the first month is:

    A. $199.
    B. $208.
    C. $216.
    D. $223.

35. Based on the information provided, the loan balance after the first month's payment will be:

    A. $198,636.
    B. $198,927.
    C. $199,462.
    D. $199,801.

36. Ashley's mortgage has a balance of $87,725. If the monthly payment is $1,225, and the house was recently appraised for $419,000, the loan-to-value ratio is equal to:

    A. 21%.
    B. 24%.
    C. 76%.
    D. 79%.

37. One discount point is equal to:

A. 1% of the interest rate.
B. 1% of the sale price.
C. 1% of the loan amount.
D. 1% of the property value.

38. If the first month's interest payment on a mortgage is $925.50, and the interest rate is 6%, the mortgage balance is:

A. $170,300.
B. $178,600.
C. $185,100.
D. $192,400.

39. If Amy borrows $250,000 and pays $2,500 quarterly in interest, then the annual interest rate on the loan is:

A. 1%.
B. 4%.
C. 6%.
D. 16%.

40. Marie purchased a house for $499,000 and obtained a mortgage for 80% of the purchase price. If the mortgage fee is 1.5%, Marie must pay:

A. $4,392.
B. $5,988.
C. $6,246.
D. $7,485.

ANSWER KEY

1. B
Step 1: Maximum mortgage = $125,000 × 3 = $375,000
Step 2: Maximum purchase price = $375,000 ÷ (1 − 0.15) = $441,176

2. C
Step 1: Annual interest = $150,000 × 0.05 = $7,500
Step 2: Monthly interest = $7,500 ÷ 12 months = $625
Step 3: Principal reduction from first payment = $805 − $625 = $180

3. B
Step 1: Katie's equity before trade = $550,000
Step 2: Jared's equity before trade = $800,000 − $150,000 = $650,000
Step 3: Difference in equity = $650,000 − $550,000 = $100,000; A fair trade requires Katie to pay Jared $100,000.

4. D
Step 1: Mortgage term = 15 years × 12 months = 180 months
Step 2: Monthly principal payment = $270,000 ÷ 180 months = $1,500
Step 3: Monthly interest rate = 0.048 ÷ 12 months = 0.004
Step 4: Monthly interest payment = $270,000 × 0.004 = $1,080
Step 5: Total monthly payment = $1,500 + $1,080 = $2,580

5. B
Step 1: Maximum annual PITI = $92,000 × 0.25 = $23,000
Step 2: Maximum monthly PITI = $23,000 ÷ 12 months = $1,916.67

6. C
Step 1: Down payment = $615,000 × (1 − 0.75) = $153,750
Step 2: Additional cash required = $153,750 − $10,000 = $143,750

7. B
Step 1: Mortgage amount = $485,000 × (1 − 0.1) = $436,500
Step 2: Amount seller will owe for points = $436,500 × 0.02 = $8,730

8. B
Step 1: Annual interest payment = $1,200 × 12 months = $14,400
Step 2: Annual interest rate = $14,400 ÷ $288,000 = 0.05 = 5%

9. C
Step 1: Monthly interest rate = 0.066 ÷ 12 months = 0.0055
Step 2: Mortgage balance = $2,104.25 ÷ 0.0055 = $382,590.91

10. B
Step 1: Monthly interest rate = 0.057 ÷ 12 months = 0.00475
Step 2: Monthly interest = $620,000 × 0.00475 = $2,945
Step 3: Total interest paid = $2,945 × 9 months = $26,505

Mortgages and Finance

11. A
Step 1: Monthly interest payable = $220,000 ÷ 12 months × 0.06 = $1,100
Step 2: Daily interest payable = $1,100 ÷ 31 days = $35.48
Step 3: The seller owned the property for 14 days (March 15 to March 28).
Step 4: Amount of interest seller owes buyer = $35.48 × 14 days = $496.72

12. B
Step 1: Down payment = $450,000 × 0.15 = $67,500
Step 2: Mortgage amount = $450,000 − $67,500 = $382,500
Step 3: PMI fee = $382,500 × 0.0075 = $2,868.75
Step 4: Origination fee = $382,500 × 0.015 = $5,737.50
Step 5: Total amount due = $67,500 + $2,868.75 + $5,737.50 = $76,106.25

13. C
Step 1: Mortgage amount = $410,000 × (1 − 0.3) = $287,000
Step 2: Amount seller will owe for points = $287,000 × 0.025 = $7,175

14. D
Step 1: Annual interest = $500,000 × 0.06 = $30,000
Step 2: Monthly interest = $30,000 ÷ 12 months = $2,500
Step 3: Principal reduction from first payment = $4,219.28 − $2,500.00 = $1,719.28
Step 4: New mortgage balance = $500,000 − $1,719.28 = $498,280.72

15. B
Step 1: Down payment = $395,000 × (1 − 0.75) = $98,750
Step 2: Additional cash required = $98,750 − $3,500 = $95,250

16. C
Step 1: Monthly interest rate = 0.054 ÷ 12 months = 0.0045
Step 2: Monthly interest = $390,000 × 0.0045 = $1,755

17. D
Step 1: Monthly interest rate = 0.054 ÷ 12 months = 0.0045
Step 2: Monthly interest = $390,000 × 0.0045 = $1,755
Step 3: Principal reduction from first payment = $2,190 − $1,755 = $435

18. B
Step 1: Mortgage amount = $130,000 × 0.75 = $97,500
Step 2: Closing costs = $97,500 × 0.02 = $1,950

19. C
Step 1: Number of payments = 30 years × 12 months = 360
Step 2: Total amount of payments = 360 × $4,691.06 = $1,688,781.60
Step 3: Total interest paid = $1,688,781.60 − $770,000.00 = $918,781.60

20. B
Step 1: Maximum mortgage = $150,000 × 4 = $600,000
Step 2: Maximum purchase price = $600,000 ÷ (1 − 0.25) = $800,000

Mortgages and Finance

21. C
Step 1: Number of payments = 20 years × 12 months = 240
Step 2: Total amount of payments = 240 × $1,922.41 = $461,378.40
Step 3: Total interest paid = $461,378.40 − $285,290.00 = $176,088.40

22. D
Step 1: Maximum annual PITI payments = $225,000 × 0.25 = $56,250
Step 2: Maximum monthly PITI payments = $56,250 ÷ 12 months = $4,687.50

23. B
Step 1: Down payment = $620,000 × (1 − 0.8) = $124,000
Step 2: Additional cash required = $124,000 − $15,500 = $108,500

24. C
Owner's equity = $1,500,000 − $600,000 = $900,000

25. B
Step 1: Owner's equity = $1,500,000 − $600,000 = $900,000
Step 2: Debt-to-equity = $600,000 ÷ $900,000 = 2:3

26. C
Step 1: Mortgage amount = $500,000 × 0.8 = $400,000
Step 2: Down payment = $515,000 − $400,000 = $115,000

27. C
Annual interest = $671,595 × 0.05125 = $34,419.24

28. A
Step 1: Monthly interest rate = 0.051 ÷ 12 months = 0.00425
Step 2: Mortgage balance = $950 ÷ 0.00425 = $223,529.41

29. D
Step 1: Annual mortgage payment = $950 × 12 months = $11,400
Step 2: Payment as a percent of income = $11,400 ÷ $88,000 = 0.13 = 13%

30. D
Step 1: Annual interest = $1,200,000 × 0.0615 = $73,800
Step 2: Monthly interest = $73,800 ÷ 12 months = $6,150

31. B
Step 1: Mortgage amount = $565,000 × 0.65 = $367,250
Step 2: Down payment = $565,000 − $367,250 = $197,750

32. C
First year interest payment = $200,000 × 0.06 = $12,000

33. A
Step 1: First year interest payment = $200,000 × 0.06 = $12,000
Step 2: First month interest payment = $12,000 ÷ 12 months = $1,000

34. A
Step 1: First year interest payment = $200,000 × 0.06 = $12,000
Step 2: First month interest payment = $12,000 ÷ 12 months = $1,000
Step 3: First month principal payment = $1,199 – $1,000 = $199

35. D
Step 1: First year interest payment = $200,000 × 0.06 = $12,000
Step 2: First month interest payment = $12,000 ÷ 12 months = $1,000
Step 3: First month principal payment = $1,199 – $1,000 = $199
Step 4: Loan balance after first payment = $200,000 – $199 = $199,801

36. A
Loan-to-value = $87,725 ÷ $419,000 = 0.21 = 21%

37. C
One discount point is equal to 1% of the loan amount.

38. C
Step 1: Monthly interest rate = 0.06 ÷ 12 months = 0.005
Step 2: Mortgage balance = $925.50 ÷ 0.005 = $185,100

39. B
Step 1: Annual interest = $2,500 × 4 quarters = $10,000
Step 2: Annual interest rate = $10,000 ÷ $250,000 = 0.04 = 4%

40. B
Step 1: Mortgage amount = $499,000 × 0.8 = $399,200
Step 2: Mortgage fee = $399,200 × 0.015 = $5,988

SECTION 4

APPRAISING REAL ESTATE VALUES

QUESTIONS

1. Richard purchased an office building for $550,000. If he collects $6,500 per month in net operating income, the capitalization rate is:

   A. 11.41%.
   B. 12.79%.
   C. 13.27%.
   D. 14.18%.

2. Alpha Realty Company is considering purchasing a building that is expected to produce annual net income of $174,000. If the company's required rate of return is 8%, the purchase price should be:

   A. $1,870,000.
   B. $1,940,000.
   C. $2,175,000.
   D. $2,215,000.

3. Al's house sustained damage in a recent tornado. If the house was worth $510,000 before the storm, and a 45% loss was sustained, the value of his house after the storm is:

   A. $229,500.
   B. $280,500.
   C. $305,000.
   D. $322,000.

4. If a house that sold for $315,000 now rents for $34,800 per year, the monthly gross rent multiplier is:

   A. 89.53.
   B. 97.74.
   C. 108.62.
   D. 121.19.

5. If the appropriate time adjustment for an 8-acre farm is an increase of 4% per year compounded annually, then the time adjustment for a comparable farm that sold for $700,000 four years ago is:

   A. $118,900.99.
   B. $119,653.08.
   C. $120,782.14.
   D. $121,461.27.

Appraising Real Estate Values

6. Monica owns a 5-year-old house that is worth $450,000. If her house has depreciated at a rate of 2% per year, the original value was:

A. $480,000.
B. $490,000.
C. $500,000.
D. $510,000.

7. Epsilon Lending Corporation is estimating the value of a 10-year-old house measuring 35 feet by 60 feet. The original cost was $95 per square foot, and depreciation is estimated to be 2% per year. If the lot is valued at $30,000, the estimated total property value is:

A. $189,600.
B. $194,300.
C. $202,700.
D. $206,400.

8. Christine's rental property produces annual gross income of $52,000. Expenses associated with the property are $15,200 per year. If the capitalization rate is 8%, the market value of her property is:

A. $190,000.
B. $460,000.
C. $650,000.
D. $840,000.

9. Delta Management Corporation provides the following data regarding cash flows for a recent capital project:

Year	0	1	2	3	4	5
Cash flow	-$95,000	$32,000	$9,000	$41,000	$45,000	$8,000

If the corporation's required rate of return is 5%, the project's net present value (NPV) is:

A. -$12,774.21.
B. -$10,305.97.
C. $19,176.83.
D. $22,346.62.

10. If the gross rent multiplier is 70, and Phil's property rents for $45,000 per year, the value of his property is:

A. $262,500.
B. $540,000.
C. $1,575,000.
D. $3,150,000.

Appraising Real Estate Values

11. Robert sold a parcel of land for $1,140,000 and made a 20% profit on the sale. The purchase price of the land was:

    A. $912,000.
    B. $950,000.
    C. $962,000.
    D. $988,000.

12. If comparable properties have been appreciating by 5% per year, a house that sold for $300,000 three years ago would be worth _____ today.

    A. $330,750.00
    B. $347,287.50
    C. $355,969.69
    D. $364,651.88

13. Theresa's investment of $1,500,000 in an apartment building produces the following cash flows:

    Year 1: $500,000
    Year 2: $600,000
    Year 3: $450,000

    If the discount rate is 6%, the investment's net present value (NPV) is:

    A. −$116,475.35.
    B. −$58,237.68.
    C. $126,201.96.
    D. $174,713.14.

14. A subject property has a gated entrance that is not present in the comparable, but the comparable has a swimming pool that the subject property does not have. The gated entrance is valued at $40,000, and the swimming pool is valued at $35,000. If the comparable recently sold for $1,200,000, the indicated value of the subject property is:

    A. $1,160,000.
    B. $1,165,000.
    C. $1,195,000.
    D. $1,205,000.

15. The current value of Brianna's house, excluding the lot, is $715,000. If her house has depreciated 3% per year for the past 5 years, the original value of her house was:

    A. $607,750.
    B. $693,550.
    C. $737,113.
    D. $841,176.

16. Raymond's investment of $1,500 in a real estate investment trust (REIT) produces the following cash flows:

Year 1: $90
Year 2: $160

If the required rate of return is 4%, the investment's net present value (NPV) is:

A. −$1,372.48.
B. −$1,265.53.
C. $1,149.84.
D. $1,309.62.

17. A comparable property that sold for $550,000 has a swimming pool ($25,000 value), third bathroom ($30,000 value), and fourth bedroom ($45,000 value) that are not present in the subject. The indicated value of the subject property is:

A. $450,000.
B. $505,000.
C. $575,000.
D. $650,000.

18. Sigma Realty Company estimates that an office building, if fully leased, would generate monthly income of $90,000. If a 5% vacancy rate is applied and the capitalization rate is 8%, the current value of the property is:

A. $10,830,000.
B. $11,645,000.
C. $12,825,000.
D. $13,910,000.

19. If the perpetual rent for a parcel is $36,600 per year, and the required rate of return on investment is 6%, the value of the parcel is:

A. $605,000.
B. $610,000.
C. $615,000.
D. $620,000.

20. Olivia sold a building for $1,900,000 and made a 25% profit on the sale. The original purchase price of the building was:

A. $475,000.
B. $1,425,000.
C. $1,520,000.
D. $2,375,000.

ANSWER KEY

1. D
Step 1: Annual net operating income = $6,500 × 12 months = $78,000
Step 2: Capitalization rate = $78,000 ÷ $550,000 = 0.1418 = 14.18%

2. C
Purchase price = $174,000 ÷ 0.08 = $2,175,000

3. B
Value after storm = $510,000 × (1 − 0.45) = $280,500

4. C
Step 1: Monthly rental income = $34,800 ÷ 12 months = $2,900
Step 2: Monthly gross rent multiplier = $315,000 ÷ $2,900 = 108.62

5. A
Step 1: Year 1 value = $700,000.00 × 1.04 = $728,000.00
Step 2: Year 2 value = $728,000.00 × 1.04 = $757,120.00
Step 3: Year 3 value = $757,120.00 × 1.04 = $787,404.80
Step 4: Year 4 value = $787,404.80 × 1.04 = $818,900.99
Step 5: Time adjustment = $818,900.99 − $700,000 = $118,900.99

6. C
Step 1: Accumulated depreciation = 5 years × 0.02 per year = 0.1
Step 2: Original value = $450,000 ÷ (1 − 0.1) = $500,000

7. A
Step 1: Square feet of house = 35 ft. × 60 ft. = 2,100 sq. ft.
Step 2: Original cost of house = 2,100 sq. ft. × $95 per sq. ft. = $199,500
Step 3: Accumulated depreciation = 10 years × 0.02 per year = 0.2
Step 4: Current value of house = $199,500 × (1 − 0.2) = $159,600
Step 5: Total property value = $159,600 + $30,000 = $189,600

8. B
Step 1: Net operating income = $52,000 − $15,200 = $36,800
Step 2: Property value = $36,800 ÷ 0.08 = $460,000

9. D
$$NPV = CF_0 + \frac{CF_1}{(1+r)^1} + \frac{CF_2}{(1+r)^2} + \frac{CF_3}{(1+r)^3} + \frac{CF_4}{(1+r)^4} + \frac{CF_5}{(1+r)^5}$$
$$NPV = -\$95,000 + \frac{\$32,000}{(1.05)^1} + \frac{\$9,000}{(1.05)^2} + \frac{\$41,000}{(1.05)^3} + \frac{\$45,000}{(1.05)^4} + \frac{\$8,000}{(1.05)^5}$$
NPV = −$95,000 + $30,476.19 + $8,163.27 + $35,417.34 + $37,021.61 + $6,268.21 = $22,346.62

10. D
Property value = 70 × $45,000 = $3,150,000

11. B
Purchase price = $1,140,000 ÷ 1.2 = $950,000

12. B
Step 1: Year 1 value = $300,000 × 1.05 = $315,000
Step 2: Year 2 value = $315,000 × 1.05 = $330,750
Step 3: Year 3 value = $330,750 × 1.05 = $347,287.50

13. A
$$NPV = CF_0 + \frac{CF_1}{(1+r)^1} + \frac{CF_2}{(1+r)^2} + \frac{CF_3}{(1+r)^3}$$
$$NPV = -\$1,500,000 + \frac{\$500,000}{(1.06)^1} + \frac{\$600,000}{(1.06)^2} + \frac{\$450,000}{(1.06)^3}$$
$$NPV = -\$1,500,000 + \$471,698.11 + \$533,997.86 + \$377,828.68 = -\$116,475.35$$

14. D
Value of subject property = $1,200,000 + $40,000 − $35,000 = $1,205,000

15. D
Step 1: Accumulated depreciation = 5 years × 0.03 per year = 0.15
Step 2: Original value = $715,000 ÷ (1 − 0.15) = $841,176

16. B
$$NPV = CF_0 + \frac{CF_1}{(1+r)^1} + \frac{CF_2}{(1+r)^2}$$
$$NPV = -\$1,500 + \frac{\$90}{(1.04)^1} + \frac{\$160}{(1.04)^2}$$
$$NPV = -\$1,500 + \$86.54 + \$147.93 = -\$1,265.53$$

17. A
Value of subject property = $550,000 − $25,000 − $30,000 − $45,000 = $450,000

18. C
Step 1: Annual potential gross income = $90,000 × 12 months = $1,080,000
Step 2: Vacancy allowance = $1,080,000 × 0.05 = $54,000
Step 3: Net operating income = $1,080,000 − $54,000 = $1,026,000
Step 4: Property value = $1,026,000 ÷ 0.08 = $12,825,000

19. B
Value of parcel = $36,600 ÷ 0.06 = $610,000

20. C
Purchase price = $1,900,000 ÷ 1.25 = $1,520,000

SECTION 5

TAXATION AND ASSESSMENT

QUESTIONS

1. Gerald's monthly mortgage payment, including principal and interest, is $900. If his annual property taxes are $7,200 and his annual homeowner's insurance premium is $600, then his monthly PITI payment is:

   A. $1,550.
   B. $1,600.
   C. $1,650.
   D. $1,700.

2. Annual property taxes of $3,600 are paid in arrears on January 1 for the previous year. Assuming 30 days per month, if the sale of the property closed on September 15, and the buyer owns the property on the day of closing, the seller will owe the buyer:

   A. $2,270.
   B. $2,540.
   C. $2,890.
   D. $3,010.

3. Sarah's house was appraised for $600,000. If the assessment ratio is 75% and taxes for the year are $13,500, the tax rate is:

   A. 15 mills.
   B. 20 mills.
   C. 25 mills.
   D. 30 mills.

4. Amanda's property has a market value of $320,000. It is assessed at 65% of value, less a $5,000 homestead exemption. If the tax rate is 30 mills, the total tax due is:

   A. $6,090.
   B. $6,240.
   C. $9,450.
   D. $9,600.

5. The Youngs, a married couple filing a joint tax return, purchased a principal residence in 2021 for $540,000. If they sold the house in 2022 for $550,000, the portion of gain subject to capital gains tax is:

   A. $0.
   B. $10,000.
   C. $250,000.
   D. $500,000.

Taxation and Assessment

6. If a property has an assessed value of $450,000 and an equalized value of $675,000, the equalization rate is:

   A. 1.25.
   B. 1.50.
   C. 1.75.
   D. 2.00.

7. There are 10 mills in:

   A. 1 cent.
   B. 10 cents.
   C. 100 cents.
   D. 1,000 cents.

8. If a property has an assessed value of $172,000, and an equalization rate of 1.2 is applied, the equalized value of the property is:

   A. $143,333.
   B. $172,000.
   C. $206,400.
   D. $344,000.

9. Renee's property was assessed at $225,400. If the millage rate is 22.5, the annual property tax is:

   A. $4,975.25.
   B. $5,071.50.
   C. $6,310.75.
   D. $7,278.25.

10. Gary is purchasing a house with a closing date of November 1. If 6 months' taxes of $5,210 were paid in advance on May 1, then Gary will owe the seller:

    A. $0.
    B. $868.
    C. $2,605.
    D. $5,210.

11. Sophia's house was recently assessed at $335,000. If the tax rate is $19 per $1,000, the annual property tax is:

    A. $6,170.
    B. $6,365.
    C. $6,840.
    D. $7,235.

Taxation and Assessment

12. If the tax rate is 20 mills, the annual tax per dollar of value is:

   A. 0.2 cents.
   B. 2 cents.
   C. 20 cents.
   D. 200 cents.

13. Emily purchased her principal residence in 2019 for $415,000. If she sold the house in 2022 for $595,000, the portion of gain subject to capital gains tax is:

   A. $0.
   B. $180,000.
   C. $250,000.
   D. $500,000.

14. Nancy's property was recently appraised for $720,000. The tax rate is 25.55 mills for the county tax and 21.35 mills for the borough tax. If the rate of assessment is 25%, the total annual property tax is:

   A. $5,809.
   B. $6,571.
   C. $7,693.
   D. $8,442.

15. The maximum exclusion of gain on the sale of a principal residence is _____ for single taxpayers and _____ for married couples filing a joint tax return.

   A. $250,000; $500,000
   B. $500,000; $250,000
   C. $500,000; $1,000,000
   D. $1,000,000; $500,000

16. A tax rate of 10 mills is equivalent to _____ for a $100,000 property.

   A. $10
   B. $100
   C. $1,000
   D. $10,000

17. Liam's property has a market value of $445,000. If the county's assessment ratio is 80% and the tax rate is 30 mills, the annual property tax is:

   A. $8,470.
   B. $9,790.
   C. $10,680.
   D. $11,240.

Taxation and Assessment

18. Eve pays $9,600 in property taxes in advance for the year on January 1. If she sells her house on September 1, the buyer will owe Eve:

    A. $1,600.
    B. $2,400.
    C. $2,800.
    D. $3,200.

19. A millage rate of 36.5 is equivalent to _____ per thousand dollars.

    A. $0.365
    B. $3.65
    C. $36.50
    D. $365.00

20. The Johnsons, a married couple filing a joint tax return, purchased a principal residence in 2017 for $680,000. If they sold the house in 2022 for $910,000, the portion of gain subject to capital gains tax is:

    A. $0.
    B. $230,000.
    C. $250,000.
    D. $500,000.

21. Barry purchased a principal residence in 2018 for $1,430,000. If he sold the house in 2022 for $1,770,000, the portion of gain subject to capital gains tax is:

    A. $0.
    B. $90,000.
    C. $250,000.
    D. $1,770,000.

22. The taxes on Dawn's property are $8,000. If the tax rate is 25 mills and the assessment ratio is 80%, the market value of her property is:

    A. $250,000.
    B. $300,000.
    C. $350,000.
    D. $400,000.

23. One mill is one dollar per _____ of assessed value.

    A. $10
    B. $100
    C. $1,000
    D. $10,000

Taxation and Assessment

24. The appraised value of Ron's house is $950,000, and the property tax is based on 35% of the appraised value. If the city tax is 30 mills and the county tax is 20 mills, the total annual property tax is:

    A. $14,575.
    B. $16,625.
    C. $18,350.
    D. $20,465.

25. Jason pays $4,800 in property taxes for 6 months in advance on April 1. If he sells his house on July 1, the buyer will owe Jason:

    A. $1,600.
    B. $2,400.
    C. $3,200.
    D. $3,800.

ANSWER KEY

1. A
Step 1: Monthly property taxes = $7,200 ÷ 12 months = $600
Step 2: Monthly insurance premium = $600 ÷ 12 months = $50
Step 3: PITI payment = $900 + $600 + $50 = $1,550

2. B
Step 1: Monthly property tax = $3,600 ÷ 12 months = $300
Step 2: Daily property tax = $300 ÷ 30 days = $10
Step 3: The seller owned the property for 8 months and 14 days.
Step 4: Amount seller owes buyer = 8 months × $300 per month = $2,400
Step 5: Amount seller owes buyer = 14 days × $10 per day = $140
Step 6: Total amount seller owes buyer = $2,400 + $140 = $2,540

3. D
Step 1: Assessed value = $600,000 × 0.75 = $450,000
Step 2: Tax rate = $13,500 ÷ $450,000 = 0.03 = 30 mills

4. A
Step 1: Assessed value = $320,000 × 0.65 = $208,000
Step 2: Adjustment for homestead exemption = $208,000 − $5,000 = $203,000
Step 3: Property tax = $203,000 × 0.03 = $6,090

5. B
Portion of gain subject to capital gains tax = $550,000 − $540,000 = $10,000
The gain on the sale is not excluded because the couple did not own the house and use it as their principal residence during at least 2 of the last 5 years before the date of sale.

6. B
Equalization rate = $675,000 ÷ $450,000 = 1.50

7. A
There are 10 mills in 1 cent.

8. C
Equalized value = $172,000 × 1.2 = $206,400

9. B
Property tax = $225,400 × 0.0225 = $5,071.50

10. A
Gary takes title to the property on the day the new tax period begins. Therefore, he owes the seller $0.

11. B
Step 1: Tax rate = $19 ÷ $1,000 = 0.019
Step 2: Property tax = $335,000 × 0.019 = $6,365

Taxation and Assessment

12. B
If the tax rate is 20 mills, the annual tax per dollar of value is 2 cents.

13. A
Portion of gain subject to capital gains tax = $0
The maximum exclusion of gain on the sale of a principal residence is $250,000 for single taxpayers who owned the house and used it as a principal residence during at least 2 of the last 5 years before the date of sale.

14. D
Step 1: Assessed value = $720,000 × 0.25 = $180,000
Step 2: County tax = $180,000 × 0.02555 = $4,599
Step 3: Borough tax = $180,000 × 0.02135 = $3,843
Step 4: Total property tax = $4,599 + $3,843 = $8,442

15. A
The maximum exclusion of gain on the sale of a principal residence is $250,000 for single taxpayers and $500,000 for married couples filing a joint tax return.

16. C
A tax rate of 10 mills is equivalent to $1,000 for a $100,000 property.

17. C
Step 1: Assessed value = $445,000 × 0.8 = $356,000
Step 2: Property tax = $356,000 × 0.03 = $10,680

18. D
Step 1: Monthly property tax = $9,600 ÷ 12 months = $800
Step 2: The buyer will own the house for 4 months.
Step 3: Amount buyer owes seller = 4 months × $800 per month = $3,200

19. C
A millage rate of 36.5 is equivalent to $36.50 per thousand dollars.

20. A
Portion of gain subject to capital gains tax = $0
The maximum exclusion of gain on the sale of a principal residence is $500,000 for married couples filing a joint tax return who owned the house and used it as their principal residence during at least 2 of the last 5 years before the date of sale.

21. B
Step 1: Gain on sale = $1,770,000 − $1,430,000 = $340,000
Step 2: Portion of gain subject to capital gains tax = $340,000 − $250,000 = $90,000
The maximum exclusion of gain on the sale of a principal residence is $250,000 for single taxpayers who owned the house and used it as a principal residence during at least 2 of the last 5 years before the date of sale.

Taxation and Assessment

22. D
Step 1: Assessed value = $8,000 ÷ 0.025 = $320,000
Step 2: Market value = $320,000 ÷ 0.8 = $400,000

23. C
One mill is one dollar per $1,000 of assessed value.

24. B
Step 1: Appraised value = $950,000 × 0.35 = $332,500
Step 2: City tax = $332,500 × 0.03 = $9,975
Step 3: County tax = $332,500 × 0.02 = $6,650
Step 4: Total property tax = $9,975 + $6,650 = $16,625

25. B
Step 1: Monthly property tax = $4,800 ÷ 6 months = $800
Step 2: The buyer will own the house for 3 months.
Step 3: Amount buyer owes seller = 3 months × $800 per month = $2,400

SECTION 6

REAL ESTATE INVESTMENT ANALYSIS

QUESTIONS

1. Helen, a property manager, receives a fee of 5% of the first $250,000 of gross rental income received, and 4% of the amount in excess of $250,000. If gross rental income is $535,000, her fee is:

   A. $21,400.
   B. $23,900.
   C. $25,300.
   D. $27,600.

2. Josh purchased an office building for $850,000. If his required rate of return is 12%, then he should charge each of his 5 tenants monthly rent of:

   A. $1,700.
   B. $1,800.
   C. $1,900.
   D. $2,000.

3. Frances purchased a property for $590,000 and resold it for $710,000. Her gross profit percentage is:

   A. 15.4%.
   B. 16.9%.
   C. 20.3%.
   D. 21.2%.

4. Ryan enters into a contract to rent a house for $2,240 per month. The first month's rent is due before moving in, along with a security deposit equal to four months' rent, plus a pet deposit equal to three months' rent. The total amount that Ryan must pay before moving into the house is:

   A. $16,840.
   B. $17,920.
   C. $18,350.
   D. $19,930.

5. Nicole would like to purchase a house that costs $835,000. If the land value is 30% of the total price, and the house is 3,450 square feet, the cost per square foot (excluding the land) is:

   A. $169.42.
   B. $197.26.
   C. $213.59.
   D. $242.03.

Real Estate Investment Analysis

6. Lucas, a real estate investor, purchased a warehouse for $885,000. If his required rate of return is 12%, the warehouse should produce monthly income of:

   A. $7,240.
   B. $7,865.
   C. $8,425.
   D. $8,850.

7. Allen purchased a commercial property for $423,000 and resold it for $517,350. His rate of profit is:

   A. 17.4%.
   B. 18.2%.
   C. 22.3%.
   D. 23.6%.

The following information relates to questions 8 – 9.
Bret, a property manager, receives compensation equal to 3% of total rent collected. Last month, total rent due was $145,000, but one tenant failed to pay his rent of $8,000.

8. Based on the information provided, Bret's compensation received for the month was:

   A. $3,910.
   B. $3,960.
   C. $4,050.
   D. $4,110.

9. Based on the information provided, Bret's compensation was _____ lower than it would have been if all the tenants had paid their rent in full.

   A. $220
   B. $240
   C. $260
   D. $280

10. Lewis, a property manager for an office building, is permitted to raise rents annually by 5% of the cost of improvements made to the building. If offices currently rent for $1,100 per month, and Lewis spends $30,000 to install an elevator, the monthly rent could be raised to:

    A. $1,125.
    B. $1,150.
    C. $1,210.
    D. $1,225.

Real Estate Investment Analysis

11. If Colin sold a property for $385,000 and made a 30% return on his investment, then his profit was:

    A. $72,583.
    B. $78,610.
    C. $84,279.
    D. $88,846.

The following information relates to questions 12 – 13.
Meredith purchased 8 lots for $20,000 each. She kept one-fourth of the lots for her personal use and sold the remaining lots for a total of $180,000.

12. Based on the information provided, the average sale price of each lot that Meredith sold was:

    A. $25,000.
    B. $30,000.
    C. $35,000.
    D. $40,000.

13. Based on the information provided, the rate of profit on each lot sold was:

    A. 35%.
    B. 40%.
    C. 45%.
    D. 50%.

14. Anthony's real estate portfolio is valued at $3,500,000 and produces gross earnings of 8%. The gross monthly return on his investment is:

    A. $20,666.
    B. $23,333.
    C. $26,000.
    D. $29,500.

15. Kristen is interested in purchasing a rental property that earns gross annual rent of $65,000. A comparable property recently sold for $900,000 that earned gross annual rent of $75,000. Using the rent multiplier method, the value of the property that Kristen is considering is:

    A. $720,000.
    B. $740,000.
    C. $780,000.
    D. $820,000.

16. Edward purchased a house for $200,000. If it earns a compounded annual return of 15%, then his property will double in value in:

    A. 3 years.
    B. 4 years.
    C. 5 years.
    D. 6 years.

17. Kappa Realty Company is considering purchasing an office building for $1,325,000. If they require an 18% return on investment, the office building should produce annual income of:

    A. $229,000.
    B. $238,500.
    C. $246,000.
    D. $252,500.

18. If a building depreciates 4% per year, its economic life is:

    A. 15 years.
    B. 20 years.
    C. 25 years.
    D. 30 years.

The following information relates to questions 19 – 21.
Linda sold 3 lots for a total of $500,000. The first lot sold for 2 times the price of the second lot. The second lot sold for 3 times the price of the third lot.

19. Based on the information provided, the first lot sold for:

    A. $200,000.
    B. $250,000.
    C. $300,000.
    D. $350,000.

20. Based on the information provided, the second lot sold for:

    A. $150,000.
    B. $200,000.
    C. $250,000.
    D. $300,000.

21. Based on the information provided, the third lot sold for:

    A. $30,000.
    B. $40,000.
    C. $50,000.
    D. $60,000.

22. If an office building depreciates 4% per year, then it will be worth 60% of its original value in:

   A. 8 years.
   B. 10 years.
   C. 12 years.
   D. 15 years.

23. Shannon owns an investment property that provides an annual pre-tax cash flow of $29,760. If the initial cash equity is $317,000, the cash-on-cash ratio is:

   A. 9.39%.
   B. 10.65%.
   C. 11.27%.
   D. 12.08%.

24. Ava purchased a house for $800,000. If she sells it 8 years later for $1,100,000, the average annual rate of appreciation is:

   A. 3.69%.
   B. 4.07%.
   C. 4.69%.
   D. 5.13%.

25. If a building's economic life is 39 years, it depreciates _____ each year.

   A. 2.56%
   B. 2.84%
   C. 3.38%
   D. 3.62%

The following information relates to questions 26 – 27.
Jill owns a building valued at $600,000. Over a 10-year period, the building has depreciated to $450,000.

26. Based on the information provided, the building depreciates _____ per year.

   A. 2.5%
   B. 3.5%
   C. 4.5%
   D. 5.5%

27. Based on the information provided, the building's useful life is:

   A. 25 years.
   B. 30 years.
   C. 35 years.
   D. 40 years.

28. Carol sold a property for $650,000, which was 125% of what she paid for it 5 years earlier. The original purchase price of Carol's property was:

A. $487,500.
B. $520,000.
C. $617,500.
D. $812,500.

29. Theta Properties purchased a lot for $150,000 and then improved it by building a parking garage valued at $900,000. The improvement ratio is:

A. 1:8.
B. 1:6.
C. 6:1.
D. 8:1.

30. Alpha Management Company owns an apartment building that has an effective gross income of $410,000 and a 7% vacancy and collection loss. If debt services are $35,000 and allowable expenses are $165,000, the net operating income is:

A. $210,000.
B. $245,000.
C. $375,000.
D. $381,000.

31. Evan purchased a house for $500,000. If the purchase price was 80% of what he sold it for 3 years later, the selling price was:

A. $400,000.
B. $550,000.
C. $575,000.
D. $625,000.

32. Abby purchased a building for $900,000. If it has a 20-year economic life, then it will be worth $225,000 in:

A. 10 years.
B. 12 years.
C. 15 years.
D. 17 years.

33. Joe purchased a building for $1,950,000. If it has a total useful life of 25 years, then its value after 11 years is:

A. $858,000.
B. $976,000.
C. $1,092,000.
D. $1,210,000.

Real Estate Investment Analysis

The following information relates to questions 34 – 36.
Delta Development Corporation is considering purchasing a building with 45,000 leasable square feet. The corporation estimates that they can rent to tenants for $25 per square foot, and the vacancy rate will be 5%. They also expect to generate $25,000 each year in additional miscellaneous income.

34. Based on the information provided, the potential gross income is:

A. $1,125,000.
B. $1,150,000.
C. $1,175,000.
D. $1,200,000.

35. Based on the information provided, the vacancy allowance is:

A. $53,000.
B. $54,500.
C. $55,750.
D. $56,250.

36. Based on the information provided, the effective gross income is:

A. $1,078,250.
B. $1,093,750.
C. $1,124,000.
D. $1,178,500.

37. Gamma Real Estate Company entered into a rental agreement that requires them to pay rent of $1,400 per month plus an additional 2% of gross annual sales exceeding $250,000. If the company's gross annual sales were $300,000 last year, the average monthly rent was:

A. $1,427.66.
B. $1,466.33.
C. $1,483.33.
D. $1,513.66.

38. Kathy is selling an apartment that is scheduled to close on April 10. She collected rent from her tenant on the first day of April in the amount of $2,700. If the buyer is due the rental income for the day of closing, Kathy will owe the buyer:

A. $810.
B. $900.
C. $1,800.
D. $1,890.

Real Estate Investment Analysis

The following information relates to questions 39 – 41.
Melissa, the property manager of a shopping center, provides the following annual data to a potential investor regarding the subject property:

Potential gross income	$850,000
Miscellaneous income	$10,000
Debt services	$125,000
Administrative expenses	$5,000
Vacancy and collection allowance	$90,000
Maintenance expenses	$15,000
Utilities	$30,000

39. Based on the information provided, the effective gross income is:

A. $680,000.
B. $710,000.
C. $740,000.
D. $770,000.

40. Based on the information provided, the net operating income is:

A. $660,000.
B. $690,000.
C. $720,000.
D. $750,000.

41. Based on the information provided, the before-tax cash flow is:

A. $545,000.
B. $570,000.
C. $595,000.
D. $620,000.

42. If a farm building has a 20-year economic life, it will depreciate _____ per year.

A. 5%
B. 6%
C. 7%
D. 8%

43. Beta Realty Company purchased an office building that currently has 17 vacancies among its 95 units. The vacancy rate is:

A. 11.2%.
B. 13.6%.
C. 15.3%.
D. 17.9%.

44. Megan, a property manager, must purchase an insurance policy to protect her property from potential liability. If a $2,000,000 insurance policy has a cost of $0.15 per $100, the annual premium is:

A. $750.
B. $1,500.
C. $2,250.
D. $3,000.

45. Kim is purchasing a house with a closing date of June 15. The homeowners' association fee of $450 is due at the beginning of each month. If Kim is charged for the day of closing, she will owe the seller:

A. $150.
B. $225.
C. $240.
D. $295.

46. Beta Development Company owns a building valued at $600,000 that has an economic life of 15 years. If the building's effective age is 5 years, and the lot is valued at $70,000, then the total current value of the property is:

A. $270,000.
B. $400,000.
C. $435,000.
D. $470,000.

47. Marcus purchased an investment property 5 years ago for $1,525,000. He made improvements of $170,000 and claimed $140,000 in depreciation. If he sells the property for $1,900,000, his capital gain is:

A. $65,000.
B. $205,000.
C. $345,000.
D. $375,000.

48. Paul owns a building that has potential gross income of $865,000 and a vacancy rate of 8%. If the building produces miscellaneous income of $20,000, the effective gross income is:

A. $815,800.
B. $825,800.
C. $845,000.
D. $885,000.

Real Estate Investment Analysis

The following information relates to questions 49 – 50.
Sigma Properties can rent out an apartment for $2,500 per month and have the tenant pay utilities, or they can rent out an apartment for $3,000 per month, but the company will pay utilities. Assume that utilities will cost $5,700 per year.

49. Based on the information provided, if the company chooses to rent out an apartment for $3,000 and pay for the utilities, the result will be:

   A. reduced revenue of $75 per month.
   B. reduced revenue of $25 per month.
   C. increased revenue of $25 per month.
   D. increased revenue of $75 per month.

50. Based on the information provided, either rental option is equally viable if utilities cost _____ per year.

   A. $5,800
   B. $6,000
   C. $6,200
   D. $6,400

51. Bryce purchased a building for $1,400,000. If it has a useful life of 25 years, then it will be worth $336,000 in:

   A. 16 years.
   B. 17 years.
   C. 18 years.
   D. 19 years.

52. Laura is a real estate investor with a required annual return of 9%. If she owns a property valued at $1,220,000, then it should produce monthly income of:

   A. $7,985.
   B. $8,640.
   C. $9,150.
   D. $10,275.

53. Jerry rents storage space that measures 20 feet by 30 feet. If the monthly rent is $700, the annual rent per square foot is:

   A. $2.
   B. $14.
   C. $17.
   D. $20.

Real Estate Investment Analysis

The following information relates to questions 54 – 55.

Sean owns an apartment complex with 11 units. Currently 4 units rent for $2,000 per month, 5 units rent for $600 per week, and 2 units are vacant. The quarterly property expenses are $16,500.

54. Based on the information provided, the net operating income is:

    A. $182,000.
    B. $186,000.
    C. $190,000.
    D. $194,000.

55. Based on the information provided, the vacancy rate is:

    A. 18%.
    B. 19%.
    C. 20%.
    D. 21%.

ANSWER KEY

1. B
Step 1: Fee on the first $250,000 = $250,000 × 0.05 = $12,500
Step 2: Fee on amount over $250,000 = ($535,000 − $250,000) × 0.04 = $11,400
Step 3: Total fee = $12,500 + $11,400 = $23,900

2. A
Step 1: Annual income = $850,000 × 0.12 = $102,000
Step 2: Monthly income = $102,000 ÷ 12 months = $8,500
Step 3: Monthly rent per tenant = $8,500 ÷ 5 tenants = $1,700 per tenant

3. C
Gross profit percentage = ($710,000 − $590,000) ÷ $590,000 = 0.203 = 20.3%

4. B
Step 1: Security deposit = $2,240 × 4 = $8,960
Step 2: Pet deposit = $2,240 × 3 = $6,720
Step 3: Total amount payable = $2,240 + $8,960 + $6,720 = $17,920

5. A
Step 1: Value of house = $835,000 × (1 − 0.3) = $584,500
Step 2: Cost per square foot = $584,500 ÷ 3,450 sq. ft. = $169.42 per sq. ft.

6. D
Step 1: Annual income = $885,000 × 0.12 = $106,200
Step 2: Monthly income = $106,200 ÷ 12 months = $8,850 per month

7. C
Rate of profit = ($517,350 − $423,000) ÷ $423,000 = 0.223 = 22.3%

8. D
Step 1: Rent collected = $145,000 − $8,000 = $137,000
Step 2: Compensation = $137,000 × 0.03 = $4,110

9. B
Reduced compensation = $8,000 × 0.03 = $240

10. D
Step 1: Annual rent increase = $30,000 × 0.05 = $1,500
Step 2: Monthly rent increase = $1,500 ÷ 12 months = $125 per month
Step 3: New monthly rent = $1,100 + $125 = $1,225

11. D
Step 1: Purchase price = $385,000 ÷ 1.3 = $296,154
Step 2: Profit = $385,000 − $296,154 = $88,846

12. B
Step 1: Lots sold = 8 lots × 3/4 = 6 lots
Step 2: Average sale price = $180,000 ÷ 6 lots = $30,000 per lot

13. D
Rate of profit = ($30,000 − $20,000) ÷ $20,000 = 0.5 = 50%

14. B
Step 1: Annual return = $3,500,000 × 0.08 = $280,000
Step 2: Monthly return = $280,000 ÷ 12 months = $23,333 per month

15. C
Step 1: Gross rent multiplier = $900,000 ÷ $75,000 = 12
Step 2: Value of property = $65,000 × 12 = $780,000

16. C
Year 1 value = $200,000 × 1.15 = $230,000
Year 2 value = $230,000 × 1.15 = $264,500
Year 3 value = $264,500 × 1.15 = $304,175
Year 4 value = $304,175 × 1.15 = $349,801
Year 5 value = $349,801 × 1.15 = $402,271

17. B
Annual income = $1,325,000 × 0.18 = $238,500

18. C
Economic life = 100% ÷ 4% per year = 25 years

19. C
Step 1: Let the third lot = Y, let the second lot = 3 × Y, let the first lot = 2 × 3 × Y
Step 2: Y + (3 × Y) + (2 × 3 × Y) = 10Y = $500,000; therefore Y = $50,000
Step 3: Selling price of first lot = 2 × 3 × Y = 2 × 3 × $50,000 = $300,000

20. A
Step 1: Let the third lot = Y, let the second lot = 3 × Y, let the first lot = 2 × 3 × Y
Step 2: Y + (3 × Y) + (2 × 3 × Y) = 10Y = $500,000; therefore Y = $50,000
Step 3: Selling price of second lot = 3 × Y = 3 × $50,000 = $150,000

21. C
Step 1: Let the third lot = Y, let the second lot = 3 × Y, let the first lot = 2 × 3 × Y
Step 2: Y + (3 × Y) + (2 × 3 × Y) = 10Y = $500,000; therefore Y = $50,000
Step 3: Selling price of third lot = Y = $50,000

22. B
Number of years = (1 − 0.6) ÷ 0.04 per year = 10 years

23. A
Cash-on-cash ratio = $29,760 ÷ $317,000 = 0.0939 = 9.39%

24. C
Step 1: Total profit = ($1,100,000 − $800,000) ÷ $800,000 = 0.375
Step 2: Annual rate of appreciation = 0.375 ÷ 8 years = 0.0469 = 4.69% per year

Real Estate Investment Analysis

25. A
Annual depreciation = 1 ÷ 39 years = 0.0256 = 2.56% per year

26. A
Step 1: Accumulated depreciation = 1 − ($450,000 ÷ $600,000) = 0.25
Step 2: Annual depreciation = 0.25 ÷ 10 years = 0.025 per year = 2.5% per year

27. D
Step 1: Accumulated depreciation = 1 − ($450,000 ÷ $600,000) = 0.25
Step 2: Annual depreciation = 0.25 ÷ 10 years = 0.025 per year
Step 3: Useful life = 1 ÷ 0.025 per year = 40 years

28. B
Original purchase price = $650,000 ÷ 1.25 = $520,000

29. C
Improvement ratio = $900,000 ÷ $150,000 = 6:1

30. B
Formula: Net operating income = Effective gross income − Allowable expenses
Net operating income = $410,000 − $165,000 = $245,000

31. D
Selling price = $500,000 ÷ 0.8 = $625,000

32. C
Step 1: Annual depreciation = 1 ÷ 20 years = 0.05 per year
Step 2: Accumulated depreciation = 1 − ($225,000 ÷ $900,000) = 0.75
Step 3: Number of years = 0.75 ÷ 0.05 per year = 15 years

33. C
Step 1: Annual depreciation = 1 ÷ 25 years = 0.04 per year
Step 2: Accumulated depreciation = 11 years × 0.04 = 0.44
Step 3: Value after 11 years = $1,950,000 × (1 − 0.44) = $1,092,000

34. A
Potential gross income = $25 per sq. ft. × 45,000 sq. ft. = $1,125,000

35. D
Step 1: Potential gross income = $25 per sq. ft. × 45,000 sq. ft. = $1,125,000
Step 2: Vacancy allowance = $1,125,000 × 0.05 = $56,250

36. B
Formula: Effective gross income = Potential gross income − Vacancy and collection allowance + Miscellaneous income
Effective gross income = $1,125,000 − $56,250 + $25,000 = $1,093,750

37. C
Step 1: Annual rent based on sales = ($300,000 − $250,000) × 0.02 = $1,000
Step 2: Monthly rent based on sales = $1,000 ÷ 12 months = $83.33 per month
Step 3: Average monthly rent = $1,400 + $83.33 = $1,483.33

38. D
Step 1: Daily rent = $2,700 ÷ 30 days = $90 per day
Step 2: The buyer will own the property for 21 days.
Step 3: Amount seller owes buyer = 21 days × $90 per day = $1,890

39. D
Formula: Effective gross income = Potential gross income − Vacancy and collection allowance + Miscellaneous income
Effective gross income = $850,000 − $90,000 + $10,000 = $770,000

40. C
Formula: Net operating income = Effective gross income − Maintenance expenses − Administrative expenses − Utilities
Net operating income = $770,000 − $15,000 − $5,000 − $30,000 = $720,000

41. C
Formula: Before-tax cash flow = Net operating income − Debt services
Before-tax cash flow = $720,000 − $125,000 = $595,000

42. A
Annual depreciation = 1 ÷ 20 years = 0.05 = 5% per year

43. D
Vacancy rate = 17 vacancies ÷ 95 units = 0.179 = 17.9%

44. D
Step 1: Premium rate = $0.15 ÷ $100 = 0.0015
Step 2: Annual premium = $2,000,000 × 0.0015 = $3,000

45. C
Step 1: Daily homeowners' association fee = $450 ÷ 30 days = $15 per day
Step 2: The buyer will own the property for 16 days.
Step 3: Amount buyer owes seller = 16 days × $15 per day = $240

46. D
Step 1: Annual depreciation = $600,000 ÷ 15 years = $40,000 per year
Step 2: Accumulated depreciation = $40,000 per year × 5 years = $200,000
Step 3: Total value of property = $600,000 − $200,000 + $70,000 = $470,000

47. C
Step 1: Total investment = $1,525,000 + $170,000 − $140,000 = $1,555,000
Step 2: Capital gain = $1,900,000 − $1,555,000 = $345,000

Real Estate Investment Analysis

48. A
Formula: Effective gross income = Potential gross income – Vacancy and collection allowance + Miscellaneous income
Effective gross income = $865,000 – ($865,000 × 0.08) + $20,000 = $815,800

49. C
Step 1: Monthly utilities = $5,700 ÷ 12 months = $475 per month
Step 2: Difference in rent attributed to utilities = $3,000 – $2,500 = $500 per month
Step 3: Increased monthly revenue = $500 – $475 = $25

50. B
Step 1: Difference in rent attributed to utilities = $3,000 – $2,500 = $500
Step 2: Utilities breakeven = $500 × 12 months = $6,000

51. D
Step 1: Annual depreciation = 1 ÷ 25 years = 0.04 per year
Step 2: Accumulated depreciation = 1 – ($336,000 ÷ $1,400,000) = 0.76
Step 3: Number of years = 0.76 ÷ 0.04 per year = 19 years

52. C
Step 1: Annual income = $1,220,000 × 0.09 = $109,800
Step 2: Monthly income = $109,800 ÷ 12 months = $9,150 per month

53. B
Step 1: Annual rent = $700 × 12 months = $8,400
Step 2: Area of storage space = 20 ft. × 30 ft. = 600 sq. ft.
Step 3: Annual rent per square foot = $8,400 ÷ 600 sq. ft. = $14 per sq. ft.

54. B
Step 1: Monthly rent in annual terms = 4 units × $2,000 per unit × 12 months = $96,000
Step 2: Weekly rent in annual terms = 5 units × $600 per unit × 52 weeks = $156,000
Step 3: Quarterly expenses in annual terms = $16,500 × 4 quarters = $66,000
Step 4: Net operating income = $96,000 + $156,000 – $66,00 = $186,000

55. A
Vacancy rate = 2 vacancies ÷ 11 units = 0.18 = 18%

SECTION 7

FUNDAMENTAL MATH CONCEPTS

QUESTIONS

1. A city is planning to repave neighborhood streets at a cost of $20 per foot of frontage. The city will pay for 60% of the cost and the homeowners must pay the remaining balance. If Mike's lot has frontage of 150 feet, and there is an identical lot directly across the street, then Mike must pay:

   A. $500.
   B. $600.
   C. $700.
   D. $800.

2. A farmer is having a cylinder-shaped silo installed that is 28 feet in diameter and 58 feet high. The volume of the cylinder is:

   A. 31,965.4 cubic feet.
   B. 33,582.9 cubic feet.
   C. 35,713.7 cubic feet.
   D. 37,824.8 cubic feet.

3. If a real estate company sold 65 houses this year and 57 houses last year, the percentage increase in houses sold is:

   A. 13%.
   B. 14%.
   C. 15%.
   D. 16%.

4. John deposited $200 in an interest-bearing account earning 5% annually. Assuming the interest is not withdrawn, the amount of interest earned in the second year will be:

   A. $10.00.
   B. $10.50.
   C. $20.50.
   D. $30.50.

5. Candace, William, and Justin are house painters. At their latest job, Candace painted 36% of the house and William painted ¼ of the house. The percentage of the house painted by Justin was:

   A. 33%.
   B. 35%.
   C. 38%.
   D. 39%.

6. If $1 is deposited in an interest-bearing account earning 7% annually, and the interest is not withdrawn, the account value at the end of 18 years will be:

   A. $3.38.
   B. $3.94.
   C. $4.26.
   D. $4.80.

7. An annual interest rate of 6.3% is equivalent to:

   A. 0.525% monthly or 1.175% quarterly.
   B. 0.525% monthly or 1.575% quarterly.
   C. 1.275% quarterly or 0.525% monthly.
   D. 2.575% quarterly or 0.525% monthly.

8. A monthly interest rate of 0.77% is equivalent to:

   A. 2.31% quarterly or 9.24% annually.
   B. 2.31% quarterly or 9.83% annually.
   C. 3.24% quarterly or 10.82% annually.
   D. 3.24% quarterly or 11.64% annually.

9. A quarterly interest rate of 1.2% is equivalent to:

   A. 0.2% monthly or 3.6% annually.
   B. 0.2% monthly or 4.8% annually.
   C. 0.4% monthly or 3.6% annually.
   D. 0.4% monthly or 4.8% annually.

10. Epsilon Corporation purchased a building and will rent out 9 floors that each measure 30,000 square feet. On each floor, 15% of the square footage must be set aside for hallways and common areas. If each office needs to be at least 1,500 square feet, Epsilon Corporation can rent a total of:

    A. 141 offices.
    B. 147 offices.
    C. 153 offices.
    D. 159 offices.

11. Aaron wants to build a rectangular log cabin with a perimeter of 200 feet. If the length of the log cabin will be 55 feet, then its width will be:

    A. 30 feet.
    B. 35 feet.
    C. 40 feet.
    D. 45 feet.

Fundamental Math Concepts

12. A crew is hired to paint a triangle-shaped section of a building's interior. If the width of the section is 44 feet and the height is 19 feet, the crew will need to paint:

    A. 418 square feet.
    B. 462 square feet.
    C. 504 square feet.
    D. 574 square feet.

13. Stephanie, a boutique owner, must pay annual rent of $10 per square foot in addition to 3% of annual gross sales exceeding $300,000. If the dimensions of the store are 40 feet by 120 feet, and $875,000 of merchandise is sold during the year, the annual rent will be:

    A. $62,250.
    B. $68,750.
    C. $74,500.
    D. $78,000.

The following information relates to questions 14 – 16.
Ben would like to build a 4-foot-high fence around his front yard. His house is 55 feet wide, and the dimensions of his front yard are 110 feet by 80 feet. The materials needed to build the fence are $15.80 per square yard and the labor cost is $13.30 per square yard. Ben estimates that each year the cost to maintain the fence will be $0.60 per square yard.

14. Based on the information provided, the cost of materials needed to build the fence is:

    A. $2,048.20.
    B. $2,282.15.
    C. $2,873.45.
    D. $3,164.60.

15. Based on the information provided, the cost of labor to install the fence is:

    A. $1,559.38.
    B. $1,682.82.
    C. $1,794.43.
    D. $1,921.05.

16. Based on the information provided, the total cost to build the fence and maintain it for the first year is:

    A. $4,289.87.
    B. $4,629.75.
    C. $4,833.49.
    D. $5,037.26.

Fundamental Math Concepts

17. The reciprocal of 1/5 can be expressed as:

    A. 1/25.
    B. 1/5.
    C. 5.
    D. 25.

18. A 12-inch by 16-inch canvas has been painted, and a 1-inch frame has been added. The area of the painting that is visible inside the frame is:

    A. 110 square inches.
    B. 120 square inches.
    C. 130 square inches.
    D. 140 square inches.

19. Jim owns an investment yielding an after-tax return of 6.2%. If he is in the 22% tax bracket, the equivalent pre-tax return is:

    A. 4.65%.
    B. 4.84%.
    C. 7.56%.
    D. 7.95%.

20. Frank's house has a triangular-shaped attic that needs to be heated. If the dimensions of the attic are 28 feet by 10 feet by 24 feet, the volume of space that needs to be heated is:

    A. 2,520 cubic feet.
    B. 2,870 cubic feet.
    C. 3,360 cubic feet.
    D. 3,930 cubic feet.

21. Housing prices have varied by the following amounts over the past 5 years: +5%, +4%, +5%, −3%, −1%. The mean, median, and mode of the data, respectively, is:

    A. 2%; 4%; 5%.
    B. 2%; 4%; −3%.
    C. 3%; −1%; 5%.
    D. 3%; 5%; −3%.

22. 10.4 feet + 15.6 inches + 8.3 yards = _____

    A. 32.4 feet
    B. 34.8 feet
    C. 36.6 feet
    D. 38.2 feet

Fundamental Math Concepts

23. Joan owns a storage warehouse that she will rent out for $0.20 per cubic foot per year. If the dimensions of the warehouse are 50 yards by 36 yards by 20 feet, the monthly rent will be:

    A. $4,600.
    B. $4,800.
    C. $5,200.
    D. $5,400.

24. An office suite has 15 employees and provides 60 square feet of work space per employee. If 5 additional employees are hired, then each employee will have their work space reduced by:

    A. 10 square feet.
    B. 15 square feet.
    C. 20 square feet.
    D. 25 square feet.

The following information relates to questions 25 – 27.
Jordan wants to install a basketball court on his property that measures 80 feet by 10 yards and is 3 inches thick. The cost of concrete is estimated to be $120 per cubic yard.

25. Based on the information provided, the volume of cubic feet of concrete needed to complete the project is:

    A. 560.
    B. 580.
    C. 600.
    D. 620.

26. Based on the information provided, the volume of cubic yards of concrete needed to complete the project is:

    A. 19.47.
    B. 20.65.
    C. 21.98.
    D. 22.22.

27. Based on the information provided, the cost of the concrete needed to complete the project is:

    A. $2,244.
    B. $2,472.
    C. $2,666.
    D. $2,891.

Fundamental Math Concepts

28. If $1 is deposited each year in an interest-bearing account earning 5.25% annually, and the interest is not withdrawn, the account value at the end of 12 years will be:

   A. $15.09.
   B. $16.15.
   C. $17.22.
   D. $18.84.

29. Mary owns an investment yielding a 7% pre-tax return. If she is in the 35% tax bracket, the equivalent after-tax return is:

   A. 2.45%.
   B. 4.55%.
   C. 9.45%.
   D. 11.55%.

The following information relates to questions 30 – 32.
Paula's income is $120,000 and she is in the 24% tax bracket. While preparing to file her tax return, she expected to take a $12,000 deduction through a government incentive program that she qualified for. However, she has discovered the deduction has been replaced with a $5,000 tax credit.

30. Ignoring exemptions and other adjustments, if Paula had claimed the $12,000 tax deduction, her total taxes owed would have been:

   A. $23,860.
   B. $24,640.
   C. $25,920.
   D. $26,080.

31. Ignoring exemptions and other adjustments, if Paula claims the $5,000 tax credit, her total taxes owed will be:

   A. $22,600.
   B. $23,800.
   C. $24,100.
   D. $25,200.

32. Ignoring exemptions and other adjustments, a tax credit of _____ would result in the same amount of taxes owed as the $12,000 tax deduction.

   A. $2,880
   B. $3,120
   C. $4,090
   D. $5,230

33. A rectangular box measuring 5.3 feet by 2.1 yards by 18 inches contains:

   A. 25.05 cubic feet.
   B. 50.09 cubic feet.
   C. 100.17 cubic feet.
   D. 200.34 cubic feet.

The following information relates to questions 34 – 37.
Jack would like to repave his driveway that is 15 feet wide, 100 feet long, and 3 inches thick. Concrete costs $90 per cubic yard and labor costs $3 per square foot.

34. Based on the information provided, the volume of concrete needed to repave the driveway is:

   A. 350 cubic feet.
   B. 375 cubic feet.
   C. 400 cubic feet.
   D. 425 cubic feet.

35. Based on the information provided, the cost of concrete needed to repave the driveway is:

   A. $1,150.
   B. $1,200.
   C. $1,250.
   D. $1,300.

36. Based on the information provided, the cost of labor to repave the driveway is:

   A. $4,500.
   B. $4,750.
   C. $5,000.
   D. $5,250.

37. Based on the information provided, Jack's total cost is:

   A. $5,000.
   B. $5,250.
   C. $5,500.
   D. $5,750.

38. The present value of $1 earning 8% interest annually for 4 years is:

   A. $0.64.
   B. $0.68.
   C. $0.70.
   D. $0.74.

Fundamental Math Concepts

39. Phillip would like to carpet a room that measures 21 feet by 27 feet. If the price of carpet is $12 per square yard, the total cost will be:

    A. $680.
    B. $756.
    C. $5,213.
    D. $6,804.

40. Colleen is installing a circular swimming pool that is 24 feet in diameter. The area of the swimming pool is:

    A. 452.39 square feet.
    B. 678.59 square feet.
    C. 904.78 square feet.
    D. 1,809.56 square feet.

ANSWER KEY

1. B
Step 1: Total cost = 150 ft. × $20 per ft. = $3,000
Step 2: Portion paid by homeowner = $3,000 × (1 − 0.6) = $1,200
Step 3: Adjustment for split cost with lot across street = $1,200 ÷ 2 lots = $600 per lot

2. C
Volume = π × r² × height
Volume = 3.1416 × 14 ft.² × 58 ft. = 35,713.7 cu. ft.

3. B
Percent change = (65 houses − 57 houses) ÷ 57 houses = 0.14 = 14%

4. B
Step 1: Year 1 value = $200.00 × 1.05 = $210.00
Step 2: Year 2 value = $210.00 × 1.05 = $220.50
Step 3: Interest earned in second year = $220.50 − $210.00 = $10.50

5. D
Percent painted by Candace: 36%
Percent painted by William: 25%
Percent painted by Candace and William: 36% + 25% = 61%
Percent painted by Justin: 100% − 61% = 39%

6. A
$S^n = (1 + i)^n$
$S^n = (1.07)^{18} = \$3.38$

7. B
Monthly interest rate = 6.3% ÷ 12 months = 0.525%
Quarterly interest rate = 6.3% ÷ 4 quarters = 1.575%

8. A
Quarterly interest rate = 0.77% × 3 months = 2.31%
Annual interest rate = 0.77% × 12 months = 9.24%

9. D
Monthly interest rate = 1.2% ÷ 3 months = 0.4%
Annual interest rate = 1.2% × 4 quarters = 4.8%

10. C
Step 1: Area for hallways and common areas = 30,000 sq. ft. × 0.15 = 4,500 sq. ft.
Step 2: Remaining area for offices = 30,000 sq. ft. − 4,500 sq. ft. = 25,500 sq. ft.
Step 3: Number of offices per floor = 25,500 sq. ft. ÷ 1,500 sq. ft. per office = 17 offices
Step 4: Total number of offices = 17 offices per floor × 9 floors = 153 offices

Fundamental Math Concepts

11. D
Perimeter = (2 × length) + (2 × width)
200 feet = (2 × 55 feet) + (2 × width)
200 feet = 110 feet + (2 × width)
90 feet = 2 × width
45 feet = width

12. A
Area = ½ base × height
Area = 0.5 × 44 ft. × 19 ft. = 418 sq. ft.

13. A
Step 1: Area of store = 40 ft. × 120 ft. = 4,800 sq. ft.
Step 2: Rent based on square footage = 4,800 sq. ft. × $10 per sq. ft. = $48,000
Step 3: Rent based on sales = ($875,000 − $300,000) × 0.03 = $17,250
Step 4: Total rent = $48,000 + $17,250 = $62,250

14. B
Conversion factor: 1 sq. yd. = 9 sq. ft.
Step 1: Perimeter to be fenced = 110 ft. + 80 ft. + 110 ft. + 80 ft. − 55 ft. = 325 ft.
Step 2: Amount of materials needed = 325 ft. × 4 ft. = 1,300 sq. ft.
Step 3: Convert to square yards = 1,300 sq. ft. ÷ 9 sq. ft. per sq. yd. = 144.44 sq. yd.
Step 4: Cost of materials = 144.44 sq. yd. × $15.80 per sq. yd. = $2,282.15

15. D
Conversion factor: 1 sq. yd. = 9 sq. ft.
Step 1: Perimeter to be fenced = 110 ft. + 80 ft. + 110 ft. + 80 ft. − 55 ft. = 325 ft.
Step 2: Amount of materials needed = 325 ft. × 4 ft. = 1,300 sq. ft.
Step 3: Convert to square yards = 1,300 sq. ft. ÷ 9 sq. ft. per sq. yd. = 144.44 sq. yd.
Step 4: Cost of labor = 144.44 sq. yd. × $13.30 per sq. yd. = $1,921.05

16. A
Conversion factor: 1 sq. yd. = 9 sq. ft.
Step 1: Perimeter to be fenced = 110 ft. + 80 ft. + 110 ft. + 80 ft. − 55 ft. = 325 ft.
Step 2: Amount of materials needed = 325 ft. × 4 ft. = 1,300 sq. ft.
Step 3: Convert to square yards = 1,300 sq. ft. ÷ 9 sq. ft. per sq. yd. = 144.44 sq. yd.
Step 4: Total cost = 144.44 sq. yd. × ($15.80 + $13.30 + $0.60 per sq. yd.) = $4,289.87

17. C
The reciprocal of a number can be found by interchanging its numerator and denominator. Therefore, the reciprocal of 1/5 is 5/1, which can be rewritten as 5.

18. D
The canvas is 12 inches by 16 inches, and after subtracting the 1-inch frame from all four sides, the dimensions inside the frame are 10 inches by 14 inches. (Remember that by subtracting 1 inch from each side you are subtracting 2 inches from the length and 2 inches from the width.) The area of the painting that is visible inside the frame can be found by multiplying 10 inches by 14 inches. 10 inches × 14 inches = 140 square inches

Fundamental Math Concepts

19. D
Pre-tax return = 0.062 ÷ (1 − 0.22) = 7.95%

20. C
Volume = ½ base × height × length
Volume = 0.5 × 28 ft. × 10 ft. × 24 ft. = 3,360 cu. ft.

21. A
Mean = [(5%)+(4%)+(5%)+(−3%)+(−1%)] ÷ 5 = 2%
Median = −3%, −1%, +4%, +5%, +5% = 4%
Mode = 5% is the only number that appears twice, therefore it is the mode.

22. C
Step 1: Convert inches to feet = 15.6 in. ÷ 12 in. per ft. = 1.3 ft.
Step 2: Convert yards to feet = 8.3 yd. × 3 ft. per yd. = 24.9 ft.
Step 3: Total length = 10.4 ft. + 1.3 ft. + 24.9 ft. = 36.6 ft.

23. D
Step 1: Convert yards to feet = 50 yd. × 3 ft. per yd. = 150 ft.
Step 2: Convert yards to feet = 36 yd. × 3 ft. per yd. = 108 ft.
Step 3: Volume = 150 ft. × 108 ft. × 20 ft. = 324,000 cu. ft.
Step 4: Annual rent = 324,000 cu. ft. × $0.20 per cu. ft. = $64,800
Step 5: Monthly rent = $64,800 ÷ 12 months = $5,400 per month

24. B
Step 1: Calculate the total area of the work space.
15 employees × 60 sq. ft. per employee = 900 sq. ft.

Step 2: Find the total number of employees.
15 employees + 5 employees = 20 employees

Step 3: Calculate the new work space area per employee.
900 sq. ft. ÷ 20 employees = 45 sq. ft. per employee

Step 4: Find the reduced area for each employee.
60 sq. ft. − 45 sq. ft. = 15 sq. ft.

25. C
Step 1: Convert yards to feet = 10 yd. × 3 ft. per yd. = 30 ft.
Step 2: Convert inches to feet = 3 in. ÷ 12 in. per ft. = 0.25 ft.
Step 3: Volume = 80 ft. × 30 ft. × 0.25 ft. = 600 cu. ft.

26. D
Conversion factor: 1 cu. yd. = 27 cu. ft.
Step 1: Convert yards to feet = 10 yd. × 3 ft. per yd. = 30 ft.
Step 2: Convert inches to feet = 3 in. ÷ 12 in. per ft. = 0.25 ft.
Step 3: Volume in cubic feet = 80 ft. × 30 ft. × 0.25 ft. = 600 cu. ft.
Step 4: Volume in cubic yards = 600 cu. ft. ÷ 27 cu. ft. per cu. yd. = 22.22 cu. yd.

Fundamental Math Concepts

27. C
Conversion factor: 1 cu. yd. = 27 cu. ft.
Step 1: Convert yards to feet = 10 yd. × 3 ft. per yd. = 30 ft.
Step 2: Convert inches to feet = 3 in. ÷ 12 in. per ft. = 0.25 ft.
Step 3: Volume in cubic feet = 80 ft. × 30 ft. × 0.25 ft. = 600 cu. ft.
Step 4: Volume in cubic yards = 600 cu. ft. ÷ 27 cu. ft. per cu. yd. = 22.22 cu. yd.
Step 5: Total cost = 22.22 cu. yd. × $120 per cu. yd. = $2,666

28. B
$S_n = [(1 + i)^n - 1] \div i$
$S_n = [(1.0525)^{12} - 1] \div 0.0525 = \$16.15$

29. B
After-tax return = 0.07 × (1 − 0.35) = 4.55%

30. C
Taxes owed from tax deduction = ($120,000 − $12,000) × 0.24 = $25,920

31. B
Taxes owed from tax credit = ($120,000 × 0.24) − $5,000 = $23,800

32. A
Step 1: Taxes owed from tax deduction = ($120,000 − $12,000) × 0.24 = $25,920
Step 2: Equivalent tax credit = ($120,000 × 0.24) − $25,920 = $2,880

33. B
Step 1: Convert yards to feet = 2.1 yd. × 3 ft. per yd. = 6.3 ft.
Step 2: Convert inches to feet = 18 in. ÷ 12 in. per ft. = 1.5 ft.
Step 3: Volume = 5.3 ft. × 6.3 ft. × 1.5 ft. = 50.09 cu. ft.

34. B
Step 1: Convert inches to feet = 3 in. ÷ 12 in. per ft. = 0.25 ft.
Step 2: Volume = 15 ft. × 100 ft. × 0.25 ft. = 375 cu. ft.

35. C
Conversion factor: 1 cu. yd. = 27 cu. ft.
Step 1: Convert inches to feet = 3 in. ÷ 12 in. per ft. = 0.25 ft.
Step 2: Volume in cubic feet = 15 ft. × 100 ft. × 0.25 ft. = 375 cu. ft.
Step 3: Volume in cubic yards = 375 cu. ft. ÷ 27 cu. ft. per cu. yd. = 13.89 cu. yd.
Step 4: Cost of concrete = 13.89 cu. yd. × $90 per cu. yd. = $1,250

36. A
Step 1: Area = 15 ft. × 100 ft. = 1,500 sq. ft.
Step 2: Cost of labor = 1,500 sq. ft. × $3 per sq. ft. = $4,500

37. D
Conversion factor: 1 cu. yd. = 27 cu. ft.
Step 1: Convert inches to feet = 3 in. ÷ 12 in. per ft. = 0.25 ft.

Step 2: Volume in cubic feet = 15 ft. × 100 ft. × 0.25 ft. = 375 cu. ft.
Step 3: Volume in cubic yards = 375 cu. ft. ÷ 27 cu. ft. per cu. yd. = 13.89 cu. yd.
Step 4: Cost of concrete = 13.89 cu. yd. × $90 per cu. yd. = $1,250
Step 5: Area = 15 ft. × 100 ft. = 1,500 sq. ft.
Step 6: Cost of labor = 1,500 sq. ft. × $3 per sq. ft. = $4,500
Step 7: Total cost = $1,250 + $4,500 = $5,750

38. D
$V^n = 1 \div [(1 + i)^n]$
$V^n = 1 \div [(1.08)^4] = \$0.74$

39. B
Conversion factor: 1 sq. yd. = 9 sq. ft.
Step 1: Area = 21 ft. × 27 ft. = 567 sq. ft.
Step 2: Convert to square yards = 567 sq. ft. ÷ 9 sq. ft. per sq. yd. = 63 sq. yd.
Step 3: Total cost = 63 sq. yd. × $12 per sq. yd. = $756

40. A
Area = π × r²
Area = 3.1416 × 12 ft.² = 452.39 sq. ft.

INDEX

A

Accumulated depreciation, 49-50, 79-81
Acre/acreage, 3-9, 11-14, 17, 19, 25-26, 45
Administrative expenses, 72, 80
After-tax return, 88, 90, 96
Allowable expenses, 70, 79
Annual interest rate, 32-33, 36, 38-39, 42, 86, 93
Annual rate of appreciation, 69, 78
Apartment, 47, 70-71, 74-75
Appraisal/appraised value, 35-37, 53, 55, 57
Area of circle, 92, 97
Area of triangle, 87, 94
Assessed value, 53-56, 59-61
Assessment ratio, 53, 55, 57
Average monthly rent, 71, 80

B

Bathroom value, 48
Bedroom value, 48
Before-tax cash flow, 72, 80
Borough tax, 55, 60

C

Capital gains tax, 53, 55-56, 59-60
Capitalization rate, 45-46, 48-49
Cash flow, 46-48, 69, 72, 80
Cash-on-cash ratio, 69, 78
City tax, 57, 61
Closing costs, 18-19, 21, 25, 34, 40
Closing date, 33, 54, 73
Commission, 17-23, 25-27
Common area, 6, 86, 93
Comparable property, 48, 67
Compounded return, 45, 68
Condo, 33
Cost of labor, 87, 91, 94, 96-97
County tax, 55, 57, 60-61

D

Daily interest, 40
Debt services, 70, 72, 80
Debt-to-equity ratio, 35, 41
Debt-to-income ratio, 31
Depreciation, 46-47, 49-50, 68-69, 72-73, 79-81
Discount points, 34, 38, 42
Down payment, 31, 33-34, 36, 39-41

E

Earnest money, 32-33, 35
Economic life, 68-69, 72-73, 78
Effective age of property, 73
Effective gross income, 70-73, 79-81
Equalization rate, 54, 59
Equalized value, 54, 59
Equity, 25, 35, 39, 41, 69
Exclusion of gain on home sale, 55, 59-60

F – G

Fair trade, 31, 39
Farm, 18, 25, 45, 72
Gross rent multiplier, 45-46, 49, 78

H – L

Home sale gain exclusion, 55, 59-60
Homeowners' association fee, 73, 80
Homestead exemption, 53, 59
Improvement ratio, 70, 79
Insurance policy, 73
Insurance premium, 53, 59, 73, 80
Interest rate, 31-40, 42, 86, 93
Investment property, 69, 73
Labor cost, 87, 91, 94, 96-97
Lease, 48, 71
Listing broker, 17, 20-21, 26
Listing salesperson, 17
Loan-to-value ratio, 36-37, 42

M

Maintenance expenses, 72, 80
Market value of property, 46, 53, 55, 57, 61
Mean, 88, 95
Median, 88, 95
Mill/millage, 53-57, 59-61
Miscellaneous income, 71-73, 79-81

Index

Mode, 88, 95
Monthly gross rent multiplier, 45, 49
Mortgage, 18, 31-42, 53

N – O

Net operating income, 45, 49-50, 70, 72, 75, 79-81
Net present value (NPV), 46-50
Office building, 22, 45, 48, 65-66, 68-69, 72
Origination fee, 33, 40
Overhead cost, 7, 14
Owner's equity, 41

P – Q

Parcel of land, 3-4, 47-48, 50
Perpetual rent, 48
Pet deposit, 65, 77
PITI payment, 31, 35, 39, 41, 53, 59
Potential gross income, 50, 71-73, 79-81
Pre-tax cash flow, 69
Pre-tax return, 88, 90, 95
Principal reduction, 39-40
Principal residence, 53, 55-56, 59-60
Private mortgage insurance (PMI) fee, 33, 40
Profit, 7, 14, 21, 27, 47-48, 65-67, 77-78
Property assessment, 53-57, 59-61
Property manager, 65-66, 72-73
Property tax, 53-57, 59-61
Proration, 33
Public Land Survey System, 8, 14
Quadrangle, 6, 13

R

Rate of profit, 21, 27, 66-67, 77-78
Real estate investment trust (REIT), 48

Referral fee, 22
Rent multiplier method, 67
Rent per square foot, 74, 81
Rental agreement, 71
Rental income, 49, 65, 71
Rental property, 46, 67
Required rate of return, 3, 45-46, 48, 65-66
Road frontage, 5, 12

S

Section, 5-6, 12-13
Security deposit, 65, 77
Selling broker, 17, 20-21
Selling costs, 7, 14
Selling salesperson, 17
Silo, 85
Subdivision, 3-4, 6
Subject property, 47-48, 50, 72
Swimming pool, 47-48, 92

T

Tax bracket, 88, 90
Tax credit, 90, 96
Tax deduction, 90, 96
Tenant, 65-66, 71, 74, 77
Time adjustment, 45, 49
Township, 5, 8, 12, 14

U – Z

Useful life of property, 69-70, 74, 79
Utilities, 72, 74, 80-81
Vacancy/vacancy rate, 48, 50, 70-73, 75, 79-81
Volume, 85, 88-89, 91, 93, 95-97
Zoning law, 7

Made in United States
Troutdale, OR
02/28/2024